SPEAKING & WRITING TRUTH

*Community Forums
on the
First Amendment*

SPEAKING & WRITING TRUTH

Community Forums on the First Amendment

ROBERT S. PECK
MARY MANEMANN
Editors

Commission on Public Understanding About the Law
American Bar Association

For further information about programs, materials and models on public understanding of the law, including those described in this book, contact:

Commission on Public Understanding About the Law, American Bar Association, 750 N. Lake Shore Drive, Chicago, IL 60611, 312/988-5725

Copyright © 1985 American Bar Association
All Rights Reserved

Produced by ABA Press
The American Bar Association
750 N. Lake Shore Drive
Chicago, IL 60611

ISBN Number: 0-897-07-203-0

CONTENTS

ACKNOWLEDGMENTS	ix
INTRODUCTION	1
CHOOSING AND USING A FORMAT	3
LIBEL	**17**
Litigating Libel: A Modern Day Zenger	19
MEMORANDUM ON LEGAL ISSUES: LIBEL	41
OBSCENITY	**53**
There's Trouble Right Here in River City	55
MEMORANDUM ON LEGAL ISSUES: OBSCENITY	66
RIGHT TO READ?	**73**
Controlling What Goes on School Library Shelves: Censorship or Selectivity?	75
MEMORANDUM ON LEGAL ISSUES: RIGHT TO READ?	87
FREEDOM OF ASSEMBLY AND GROUP LIBEL	**91**
Nazis March on Libertyville	93
MEMORANDUM ON LEGAL ISSUES: FREEDOM OF ASSEMBLY AND GROUP LIBEL	105
NATIONAL SECURITY AND THE PRESS	**113**
Publishing the Nation's Secrets	115
MEMORANDUM ON LEGAL ISSUES: NATIONAL SECURITY AND THE PRESS	131
REPORTERS' SHIELD LAWS	**145**
A Case of Confidentiality	147
MEMORANDUM ON LEGAL ISSUES: REPORTERS' SHIELD LAWS	155
THE ZENGER TRIAL: ITS BEGINNINGS AND LEGACY	**161**
Speaking and Writing Truth, *Robert S. Peck*	163

About the Authors

ROBERT S. PECK is staff director of the American Bar Association's Commission on Public Understanding About the Law and director of the ABA's project to celebrate the bicentennial of the Constitution. He has written extensively on constitutional issues in law reviews, magazines and newspapers. He is former legal director of the Public Education Association in New York City. Prior to his legal career, Mr. Peck worked as a journalist and as a congressional aide.

MARY MANEMANN is staff assistant for the American Bar Association's Commission on Public Understanding About the Law. Since arriving at the ABA, she has worked on projects related to the constitutional bicentennial and written articles for publications like *Passport to Legal Understanding* and *Update on Law-Related Education*. Ms. Manemann is a recent graduate of Northwestern University's Medill School of Journalism.

Acknowledgments

> ...*Instead of dating American Liberty from the Stamp Act,...[it can be traced] to the persecution of Zenger; Because that event revealed the philosophy of freedom, both of thought and speech, as an inborn human right, so nobly set forth in Milton's speech for the "Liberty of Unlicensed Printing."*
> — Justice Steele, Colorado Supreme Court, dissenting in a 1906 seditious libel case.

It is always a special pleasure to be involved in a project concerned with certain timeless principles, like freedom of speech and freedom of the press. No matter how much you have studied the subject, you are constantly treated to new revelations, insights and the excitement that comes from the process of learning and understanding. We particularly feel that way about this project.

This book is but one step toward a proper celebration of the U.S. Constitution's 200th anniversary — a celebration that should be feted by reacquainting ourselves with principles that justify our pride in our country. It was funded by grants from the UPS Foundation, the General Foods Foundation, and the American Bar Endowment. We thank these generous supporters for helping the American public examine and better understand our constitutional system.

We wish also to express our gratitude to the many people who made this book possible: Melissa L. Zox, who researched and wrote various sections while working as a student intern in our office; Charles J. White, III, who gave us the benefit of his experience as publications director of the ABA's Public Education Division and helped see us through to production; Harvey Retzloff, who designed the book; Belinda Ewing, who patiently typed the word processing codes from which it was automatically typeset; May Nash, who in a flash always produced photocopies and files of whatever we requested; Vicki Quade of the ABA Press, who helped proofread and edit; and Donna Tashjian and Jerry Hutchins of the ABA Press, who are responsible for the cover design.

We hope you will find this book a useful tool in planning, studying and inspiring public understanding of our constitutional system and the citizen's unique role in making that system work.

Robert S. Peck
Mary Manemann
ABA Commission on Public
Understanding About the Law

August 1985

INTRODUCTION

In 1987, Americans will celebrate the 200th anniversary of the United States Constitution. That achievement is a significant one, for it represents a popular respect for the rule of law in governing our society and settling our common disputes. Unfortunately, while citizens love their Constitution in the abstract, most know very little about what it actually says or why it says what it does. They often lack any background in its history or the political theory behind it. Moreover, they fail to realize its continuing importance in American life except on those occasions when the Supreme Court, in Olympian fashion, surprises the public by declaring a popular governmental action unconstitutional.

The lack of public understanding about our constitutional system is unhealthy—unhealthy because when the citizens do not understand the most basic of our laws they lose respect and confidence in the value of laws and in the legal system itself. In a society such as ours, citizens are regularly called upon to make judgments about national and local issues, most of which involve some aspect of law. Widespread public ignorance of the law and its importance represents a weakness and a potential danger to our constitutional system.

The Constitution's bicentennial presents an historic opportunity to direct public attention to the Constitution and the important American values it represents. Through educational programs, the public can learn more about the important role the average citizen plays in our constitutional system and be better prepared to fulfill the obligations reserved for that high office. By making the bicentennial a learning experience for the nation, we have an opportunity to rededicate ourselves to the ideals that are the source of our pride in our traditions and our uniquely American heritage—a heritage that allows all of us, from those who trace their ancestry to colonial America to the most recently naturalized citizen, to claim a strong kinship to the Founding Fathers and the ideal of liberty they sought to establish.

This handbook helps organizations that are preparing to celebrate the bicentennial through community and school events to begin work with forums on First Amendment issues of freedom of speech and of the press. The forums are designed to educate the audience in constitutional principles by allowing them to speak out on the First Amendment issues featured in the project. The forums also emphasize the citizen's role in the continuing development of law, through discussions on issues of contemporary and everyday importance.

As Justice Louis Brandeis wrote, concurring in *Whitney v. California*, 274 U.S. 357, 375-76 (1927): "Those who won our independence believed... that public discussion is a political duty; and that this should be a fundamental principle of the American government." The forums take this principle to heart, giving citizens an opportunity to discuss the constitutional questions of our time.

The First Amendment focus of these initial forums was chosen to commemorate an important anniversary in the struggle for liberty: the 250th anniversary of the acquittal of colonial publisher John Peter Zenger on charges of seditious libel. The final chapter of this book relates the story of that trial. The forums examine the United States' free speech/free press heritage and its relevance in contemporary life. They may be supplemented by other locally initiated events that encourage recognition of the continuing importance of the Zenger legacy. While the forums represent a prefabricated model for public programs on the First Amendment, they also present local sponsors with an opportunity for further creativity in the subject area. The information presented here can also be the subject of articles, publications, conferences and speeches, to give just a few examples. Whatever means are chosen to convey the rich constitutional heritage we enjoy as Americans, the American Bar Association's Commission on Public Understanding About the Law remains ready to assist.

CHOOSING AND USING A FORMAT

Choosing a Format

Four basic forum formats were developed to combine brief concept presentations with frequent opportunities for the audience to participate in dialogue with discussion leaders, who will often be scholars in the subject area. By structuring the forums carefully, organizers will ensure they serve their educational purpose, as well as give participants an opportunity to explore constitutional considerations that are conceptually new to them. The forums will also be local news events, generating their own coverage and further educational outreach.

Organizers may choose from the following model formats: *mock legislative hearing, town hall meeting (socratic discussion), mock trial,* and *debate*. These format options ensure that local needs, resources and abilities are best utilized.

Mock Legislative Hearing

The *legislative hearing* format follows the formula successfully used by the ABA and the National Community Education Association (NCEA) in a National Endowment for the Humanities planning grant project called "The First Amendment in Our Daily Decision-Making." The project was tested in San Diego, California, and Raleigh-Durham, North Carolina, in 1982 and 1983. The same format was later used in New Orleans at Communications Expo '84 of the National Association of Bar Executives, a professional association of state and local bar association executives.

The San Diego program exemplifed the format of the forums. It featured a mock town council meeting as a means of addressing key First Amendment issues. The major local co-sponsors were the San Diego County Department of Education (affiliated with the NCEA), the San Diego County Bar Association, the San Diego Community College District, and the University of San Diego. Other community groups, including the League of Women Voters and senior citizens' groups, were also involved in planning and building an audience for the event. Prominent local citizens played leading roles in the forum, helping attract the audience. The meeting was videotaped for future use in classrooms and on the local cable television station.

At the forum, mock council members introduced several resolutions with implications for First Amendment concerns. The resolutions addressed real community issues. Council members heard testimony from witnesses planted among the audience. As prearranged, the testifying "witnesses" represented all points of view. Since even those with prepared scripts seemed to come up from the audience voluntarily, other members of the audience also took up the invitation to speak to the issues. The forum was capped by a review of relevant law by the council's "legal counsel." Participants were then polled on the questions debated and the value of the forum as an educational device about the First Amendment.

Town Hall Meeting

The other forum formats similarly mix the educational and participatory elements found in the mock legislative hearing. The *town hall meeting* format might best be described as similar to those which television talk shows hosts use to encourage dialogue between the audience and a panel of experts. It features a moderator and expert guests, who can present a constitutional issue of contemporary importance, draw on historic and social influences pertinent to the issue, and place the issue in the larger context of American society. Members of the audience are encouraged to question the experts and respond to the discussion. A socratic dialogue ensues, where the knowledgeable moderator tests the audience's opinions through hypothetical situations that apply their beliefs to unforeseen circumstances. The expert guests should be carefully selected to represent responsibly all viewpoints and give the issue a full and fair hearing.

The key to success in this format is choosing the right moderator to serve as discussion leader. The person should be familiar with the subject matter, capable of putting the audience at ease and something of a showman. Many law school professors have experience and ability in using the socratic method to elicit discussion and debate from a large group. This kind of experience may be ideal for a large public audience. Local sponsors may wish to look to neighboring law schools for a discussion leader. Still, it is important to remember the differences between a class of law students and a lay adult audience. To keep the audience interested, you need a measure of "entertainment" in the proceedings and a clear presentation that avoids legalisms. Some very effective law professors may not necessarily be effective as discussion leaders in this program.

Local sponsors should consider other possible candidates for moderator. For example, public officials, including judges, may be approached; so may local radio or television talk show hosts who have experience with the format and can use the experts to fill in gaps in their own knowledge. Choosing a well-known local personality may be very useful to promote the program and attract an audience.

Mock Trial

In the *mock trial* format, the audience will witness the drama of issues presented in a courtroom trial or appellate hearing, designed to raise all relevant questions and present intensive advocacy from both sides of the issues. The audience will then serve as jurors, discussing the testimony and choosing the result they believe proper. The judge, much like the moderator in the town hall format, will lead the audience discussion (jury deliberation) in a socratic dialogue. The trial participants will also be available to help guide this discussion.

Debate

Finally, a *debate* format gives sponsors a less elaborate alternative for the forums. The debate should feature prominent advocates and be followed by a question-and-answer period, during which members of the audience direct inquiries to the debaters and then discuss the points raised. Here again, an experienced discussion leader is important to making the audience participation meaningful.

All of the formats are well-suited to the use of media. Videotaped or filmed segments may be incorporated into presentations. The "council meeting" may be broadcast on local radio, television or cable to reach a larger, more general audience. Broadcast live, the formats permit a listening audience to participate by telephone, calling in opinions and votes. Videotaped, the programs may be used by schools and other community groups as the basis for later educational efforts.

The scripts and the legal memos are specifically designed for use at the *mock legislative hearings* and the *mock trials*. However, the information they contain can be applied toward planning *town hall meetings* or *debates*.

Goals. The forums are designed to further the following goals for their participants:
1. To acquire knowledge of First Amendment principles;
2. To observe the practical application of abstract legal principles to issues of local concern;
3. To recognize the diverse social, moral and economic values that are central to legal issues;
4. To observe the ways in which law expresses community values;
5. To observe the law used as a tool in resolving issues and accommodating different interests; and
6. To understand the citizen's continuing role in the development of the law.

Planning a Forum

In executing any of the formats, attention must be given to scheduling, space requirements, topics, speakers, audience, and public relations. Forming a committee, with each of its members assigned one of the major responsibilities listed above, can assure that the forums will be successfully implemented. Committee members may include representatives of the legal profession, the education community, the media, and other community organizations. This broad representation from diverse occupations can help later with publicity, acquiring speakers, and attracting an audience. The committee should be large enough to accomplish the tasks to be undertaken. Each person on the committee should keep written records to be circulated among the members, attend regular committee meetings and receive continuous follow-up and reinforcement.

Scheduling

Scheduling should be one of the first steps the committee addresses. It is often easier to schedule the forums around special voluntary, club or group activities. The forums can be held at regular meeting times and locations when associated with a special group. Scheduling forums in this manner guarantees them an audience. If possible, the group's meeting should be open to the public, to build a larger audience on the established base of the group's membership.

If a general audience is preferred, then the forums must be presented on a weekend day or a weekday evening. Saturday mornings are the best time to attract a large audience, according to many bar associations.

Finding Space

Scheduling often hinges on the space available. For audiences that will come from an existing organization, the group's regular meeting space would be appropriate. For a general audience, local schools or community colleges offer possible locations, but using them may require attendees to register for a course or organizers to make a large monetary deposit as liability insurance. For schools and other public buildings like shopping centers, appropriate county, city, and state officials must be contacted to obtain permission and, possibly, a permit. Dealing with any bureaucratic tangles should be done well in advance, since it can be a time-consuming process. In choosing a location, look for a central site near public transportation with parking facilities, security and several rooms to allow for smaller discussion groups. If you expect a large audience, provide a proper sound system, with a back-up system if possible. These should be secured and tested in advance.

Before you begin actively searching for a location, consider possible spaces that might be donated or involve only minimal cost. Remember, even using "free" public or private space may still require a security deposit. With any space, obtain a written document that clarifies the terms of your agreement and protects the rights of forum organizers.

Deciding on Topics and Choosing a Format

To select your topic, use the forums provided here: either in their entirety or as guides to other approaches. For a specialized audience, a special topic may be selected. Also, organizers can survey the target audience to collect subject ideas. The topic and format should be geared toward the individual community. If a particular issue has stirred up local controversy or interest, then it might be a ripe topic for a forum. In choosing a topic, aim to attract the audience's interest and, for most formats, their participation.

The format you select depends on the participants who are available. When two well-known individuals can tackle the two sides of an issue, using the debate format might be the best bet. If you have an ample supply of players, the mock legislative hearing or mock trial formats are natural choices. An especially exciting moderator and a wealth of true expertise may indicate the town hall format would be a feasible option. In any event, if the audience appears too timid to participate voluntarily, be prepared to turn whatever format you choose into a socratic discussion. This will encourage the audience to get involved.

Selecting Participants

You can choose participants from a variety of sources. Obviously, members of the bar and educators offer many possibilities, as do members of the co-sponsoring public organizations. Participants who are familiar with the viewpoints they will propose in the roles they play can add invaluable knowledge, persuasiveness and realism to the proceedings.

Planning groups may also have local public officials play the roles that correspond to their offices. Several important cautions must be considered, however. The issues discussed in these forums were chosen for their popular interest, currency and controversy. Public officials may be reluctant to speak freely on hypothetical issues that they may have to take future action on. In addition, organizers must be sensitive to possible charges of favoritism when using public officials in an election year. Wisdom might dictate that you avoid using any political candidates, unless all are represented. Nonetheless, having local officials participate in these programs offers immense potential and should be carefully considered.

Local sponsors should also use caution before inviting representatives of actual interest groups to participate as players. These representatives can contribute realism and enthusiasm to their presentations, particularly if they advocate positions similar to those in the instructional materials, but they may get carried away by the soapbox a community forum would give them. The dangers they pose may outweigh the benefits, and the controversial nature of the proposals could overshadow the forums' function as vehicles for instruction on the Constitution.

After the committee targets several potential participants, contact them early in the forum's planning stages since many must work around tight schedules.

Once your aspiring actors accept the invitation to participate, send them more information and a forum script. One or several meetings with the participants and the committee may be needed to clarify their roles and to answer questions. In some instances, rehearsing in front of the committee may be beneficial. The number of meetings and the type of contacts you have with forum participants (i.e., in person, by letter, or by phone) will depend on the commitments and time constraints of both participants and committee members. In any case, maintain some sort of continuous contact to ensure a smooth and successful production.

Acquiring an Audience

The format and the nature of issues in each forum are particularly attractive for adults, but they may be used with equal success before student audiences. The major responsibility for attracting the audience rests on the sponsoring organizations. Use the coalition committee that planned the forums as a building block for a larger audience, with its base each group's constituents. Committees should seek additional sponsors in local civic, fraternal, service or other such organizations early in the planning process.

Additional sponsors can help in a number of ways. Their membership can serve as the nucleus of the audience. They are also a source of volunteers for promotion and production and a pool for active participants. The groups' prestige will aid in promotion and in seeking financial support. Their participation also ensures that a developing program remains properly geared to a lay audience. Senior citizens' groups, in particular, are promising candidates as co-sponsors. Their members have time, interest, and a wealth of experience in different areas, all of which can be invaluable in planning, producing and conducting the program.

Developing an effective promotional strategy is essential to reach out to the community. This can be achieved by involving local press, and radio and television stations, who could aid the project through general community interest. They may also want to increase public understanding of issues they find particularly attractive, most notably freedom of the press. In addition, the media might see opportunities for original local programming based on the project. For example, local educational or cable television may become co-sponsors with the intent of presenting sessions live or videotaped. This kind of media involvement offers many opportunities for production assistance, financial contributions, promotion and publicity.

Promoting the Forum

As the planning process proceeds, a concentrated effort needs to be placed on public relations. For a specific group-related audience, the organization can advertise during meetings and in available publications or newsletters. To attract a general audience, the media can be helpful.

To make sure accurate and useful information will be publicized, the committee should prepare a press release with the who, what, where, when and why of the forum. Informational materials should include the names of speakers; questions to be addressed; time, date, and location of the seminar; and sponsors of the program. News releases should be mailed or delivered to local newspapers, radio and television stations, as well as to weekly newspapers, which usually publish on Wednesdays and Thursdays. All news items must be distributed at once, so that each media outlet receives equal treatment. Prepare at least two news releases before the forums. One should announce the what, where and when of the event before the names of all panelists are finalized; the second release should identify the panelists and repeat the earlier information. Contact radio and television stations about the possibility of having your panelists appear on talk shows before the forums. Select an articulate spokesman from your planning group, who can arouse interest and build attendance by describing your plans. Many radio and television stations will also assist you by taping public service announcements.

Other effective ways to advertise the forums include posting signs in prominent public locations like grocery stores, libraries, and shopping malls; distributing free pamphlets or flyers, similar to the press release, that provide detailed information; and mailings and telephone calls to those identified as potential participants.

On the night planned for your presentation, make sure you post maps and signs to help people find the forum. Outlines of the forum scripts and pamphlets from local or state bar associations may make good handouts. Programs with the speakers, titles and subjects to be presented should be available. If possible, have ushers welcome the audience and guide them to their seats, giving out programs and other materials and collecting questionaires.

At the forum, set out a registration desk with nametags and a guest book. Nametags involve the audience by allowing them to address each other by name. The guestbook can be used to identify attendees, so that they can be mailed information about future seminars and follow-up surveys on the forum.

These sample promotional materials can be adapted to suit your local needs:

Sample Letter for Service and Civic Organizations in Your Community

                                                         (date)

Dear _____:

Constitutional issues are a part of our daily lives, even if we don't always realize their importance. On _____ (date), a free public seminar will be held on the First Amendment, specifically to explore issues relating to _____
(topic to be addressed in forum).
Your members are welcome to participate and share in a discussion of these important issues, while learning more about the citizen's role in our constitutional system of government.
The seminar is sponsored by _____
(names of organizations).
In 1985, we celebrate the 250th anniversary of the seditious libel trial of colonial publisher John Peter Zenger, a trial that helped establish in America the principles that were later embodied in the First Amendment. Zenger was tried not because what he published was false, but because it offended the colonial governor. His acquittal by a jury was an important step in the development of freedom of the press. Help us celebrate this event by exercising your freedom of speech at the forum.
The forum is designed in a format geared toward audience participation. Throughout the country, state-level committees have been organizing similar forums. Our entire membership is supporting this endeavor, and we invite the interest of your organization and its members.
The forums will be held on _____ (dates of seminar), at _____ (time of seminar). It will be held at
_____ (name and location).
Thank you for assisting us in making sure all the people in this area are aware of our constitutional forums.

                                      Sincerely,

                                      _____ (name)
                                      _____ (title)

                                      _____
                                      (telephone number)

Radio and television public service announcements (both 30-second and 60-second spots) that stations in your area can air at no charge:

30-Second Public Service Announcement

The _____ (sponsoring organization) is giving area residents an opportunity to learn more about the way the First Amendment affects them every day, using controversies about free speech, free press, and the legal issues involved. On _____ (date), you are invited to attend a free public forum on _____ (topic), _____ (place and location) at _____ (time). A distinguished group of community leaders, including representatives from the media and the legal profession, will be available to join you in discussing the issues. For more information call the _____ (organization) at _____ (telephone number).

60-Second Public Service Announcement

Have you ever wondered about _____ (topic)? You'll get a chance to express your views and receive some answers to your questions at a free public forum on _____ (date), sponsored by the _____ (organization) from _____ to _____ (times) at _____ (location). Open to the public, the seminar will use the expertise of a panel of experts from the media and the legal profession to explore current First Amendment issues. It will look at a hypothetical case involving controversial free speech and free press issues, featuring _____ _____ (longer description of topic). You'll get a chance to question points of law, and to acquire a better understanding of the Constitution and your rights and responsiblities under the law. Call the _____ (organization) for more information, at _____ (telephone number).

Sample News Release

FROM: (name of sponsor)   CONTACT: (name of chairman, address, phone)

FREE PUBLIC FIRST AMENDMENT   FOR IMMEDIATE RELEASE
FORUM SCHEDULED

(City, Date) Citizens can discuss current—and perhaps controversial—First Amendment issues at a public forum sponsored by _____ _____ (organization) on _____ (date) at _____ (time) p.m. It will take place at _____(location). This event helps commemorate the 250th anniversary of the seditious libel trial of colonial printer John Peter Zenger, who was acquitted by using truth as a defense. The Zenger trial is part of the American legacy of freedoms of speech and press, embodied in the First Amendment to the U.S. Constitution.

The forum uses a hypothetical case to examine the First Amendment issue of _____ (topic), with _____

(the scenario and further explanation of your particular forum).
The forum will make use of local experts from various fields, featuring representatives of the media and legal profession. They include:

_____
_____
_____
_____
_____

(a list of the participants).
For more information about the forum, contact _____ (name), at _____ (telephone number).

Polling the Audience

You might find it helpful to conduct pre-forum and post-forum surveys. At the registration desk, the audience should be provided with surveys to complete and pass in before the forum begins. Questions can determine what level of knowledge they already have on the issue, any preconceived notions about the forum or the issue to be presented, and any previous experience in this sort of learning experience. Routine questions asking sex, age, and occupation should be included as well.

The post-forum survey can be provided with the information package received at registration, handed out at the end of the forum or sent by mail shortly after the event. Distributing the survey sometime during the event ensures a better return rate and immediate impact, as well as saving money on postage. This post-forum poll should ask what participants learned from the experience, if their expectations were fulfilled, suggestions for future forums and whether they would be interested in attending a future forum.

After the forum, the committee should meet to send thank-you notes to key participants and to evaluate the feedback they received. This follow-up evaluation should take place while experiences from the forum are still fresh in committee members' minds. After assessing the forum, committee members can also decide on the desirability of holding future forums on other subjects.

Suggestions for Forum Surveys

Pre-Forum Survey

Please answer all questions as completely as possible. Personal information is optional. All answers will be confidential. Thank you for helping us evaluate our efforts.

How did you hear about the forum?

Was the location easily accessible?
    Yes _____ No _____

Was the time, the day, and the date convenient?
    Yes _____ No _____

If not, what would have been preferable? _____

Do you have any previous experience with public forums?
    Yes _____ No _____

If so, where? _____

Who was the sponsor? _____

What topic(s) was (were) covered? _____

Do you have previous experience with the topic being discussed today?
    Yes _____ No _____

If so, in what context? _____

Why did you attend the forum today?

(Include specific questions about participants' opinions on the issue to be discussed. Use the following examples as a guide.)

Do you think newspapers should be required by law to publish corrections of errors in articles they publish?
    Yes _____ No _____

When a newspaper is sued for libel, should it matter that they honestly believed what they published was true and was important information for the public to know?

Yes _____ No _____

Do you believe that newspapers are:

_____ responsible and fair in their reporting.

_____ sometimes responsible, sometimes irresponsible.

_____ sensational and biased.

Should televison be treated differently, for First Amendment purposes, from newspapers and other publications?

Yes _____ No _____

Name (optional): _____

Address (optional): _____

_____

Sex: female _____ male _____

Occupation: _____

Age: _____

Post-Forum Survey

Please answer these questions in as much detail as possible. Personal information is optional. All answers will be confidential. Your response will help assess both this forum's successes and its weaker points. Thank you for attending.

Were your expectations for the forum fulfilled?

Yes _____ No _____ Sort of _____

Why?

Did you feel comfortable enough to participate?

Were the facilities appropriate?

Was the presentation realistic?

What key points did you learn?

What was missing in the forum?

How could the forums be more interesting?

Was the topic stimulating?

Were the presenters stimulating?

What other topics would you find interesting?

(Include specific questions about the issue discussed at the forum, to be compared to the audience's perceptions before the forum. Use the following examples as guides.)

Should the government be able to ban pornography in a certain part of the community if the people support such action?
    Yes _____ No _____

Would a proposal banning a magazine like *Playboy* be unconstitutional?
    Yes _____ No _____

What kinds of obscene materials do you believe can and should be regulated within the confines of First Amendment requirements?
    _____ Words that describe obscene behavior
    _____ Photographs or illustrations that portray obscene behavior
    _____ Movies
    _____ None of the above

Would you like to be contacted if there are future forums?
    Yes _____ No _____

Name (optional): _____

Address (optional): _____

Sex: female _____ male _____

Occupation: _____

Age: _____

LIBEL

Litigating Libel:
A Modern Day Zenger

Cast of Characters, in order of their appearance

GLEN JENCKS, Calhoun County Court Judge
BRIAN MICHAELSON, attorney for the plaintiff
SHIRLEY KING, counsel for the defendant
ORVILLE NOTTINGHAM, plaintiff and state governor
GARRISON KILEY, captain of a National Guard unit
JANICE EBERHARDT, a Western State University student
GLORIA WRIGHT, defendant and reporter for *The Vigilant*
JEREMY BENTHAM, a Western State University student

This mock trial examines libel as it applies to public officials. Forum organizers should rehearse witness-participants beforehand. The audience will serve as jurors. The trial relates to an article that appeared in a newspaper known as *The Vigilant*, written by journalist Gloria Wright. The article appears in its entirety on the following pages. Forum organizers should reproduce and distribute it to both participants and the audience for reference during the trial.

The Vigilant
—Forever the Guardian of Freedom—

October 15, 19___

Two-fold Tragedy Tears Campus

Mounting evidence indicates that the tragic shooting of two student protesters at Western State University earlier this week was the natural consequence of orders issued by Governor Orville Nottingham. The October 10 tragedy has already ignited an intense debate about the propriety of the governor's actions—and how much responsibility he bears for the deaths of students Patricia Renicke and Frank Waldman.

When he called out the National Guard to Western State to contain the students' anti-apartheid demonstration, Nottingham set up the scenario that led directly to the students' deaths. Guardsmen present to receive the governor's orders quote him as saying they should "give those kids a good spanking." Renicke and Waldman were killed by National Guardsmen as they demonstrated peacefully against the American business-as-usual attitude in racist South Africa.

The Guardsmen had already been alarmed by reports from the governor's office that the protest was sure to turn radical. Agents of the governor had blanketed the campus in advance of the demonstration and returned with exaggerated reports of planned violence.

"Intelligence showed radical groups were bent on creating a violent symbol to draw attention to their cause," said Garrison Kiley, captain of the Guard unit sent to Western State. "When we went to Whittier, our latest reports claimed these radical groups were steadily amassing strength."

While the Guardsmen were told they were up against an unruly group of anarchists, several students intimately acquainted with the goals of the demonstration say the governor led the Guard astray. According to Jeremy Bentham, a Western State sophomore involved in planning the demonstration, intelligence agents for the governor appeared on campus a week before the planned protest. Bentham said the agents talked to most groups participating in the planning, but they soon lost their focus.

"They [government agents] became obsessed with a splinter group known as the Alliance for the Oppressed," Bentham said. "After a while, they ignored the more moderate student groups, although we were then really in control of how the protest would go."

Bentham hypothesized that the Alliance's punk attire and radical philosophies made them an easier enemy for the government.

"It was a lot easier to wage war against what seemed to be a bunch of deviants than to punish kids who looked as if they lived next door," Bentham said. However, he claims Nottingham's approach backfired.

"What the governor's agents did with the Alliance is exactly what people complain the media does with international terrorists," said Bentham. "All of the attention made them seem more significant than they really were. Eventually it succeeded in *making* them more significant. When the Guard arrived the day of the demonstration, a lot of students came to the quick conclusion that they should have been listening to the Alliance all along. Nottingham and his staff helped fulfill their own prophecy."

Governor Nottingham has often aroused the ire and dismay of those who claim his policies are reactionary — or just plain wrong. Sources in the capital also say the governor has repeatedly linked today's campus campaigns against apartheid with protests of the 1960s. During his first gubernatorial race, Nottingham lashed out at student protesters as "idlers" and "no-accounts who were destroying the morale of the campuses and of the country."

Nottingham's actions at Western State carry on this paranoia for disaffection with established policies. Moreover, today's student concerns over the problems inherent in American economic support of the South African apartheid regime hit too close to home for him to ignore.

Nottingham owns a controlling interest in Sierra Mining, the principal U.S. connection to the South African diamond industry. While it has long been known that this ownership accounted for the governor's wealth, the passage last year of the new "Ethics in Government" Act forced Nottingham to reveal that he owned stock in a number of corporations with interests in South Africa. Students targeted Nottingham in their protest at Western State because of his South African holdings. Any change in U.S. policies toward South Africa would profoundly affect Nottingham's private finances. Some say his use of the National Guard was less concerned with quelling potential violence than protecting his personal fiefdom.

In his actions at Western State, Nottingham merely continued what have become his customary policies. This time, however, they led to a bloody conclusion. He broke his pledge to the people to uphold and defend the laws of the land and broke those very laws himself. By denying the students the opportunity to speak out on their political beliefs at Western State, Nottingham violated their constitutional right of freedom of speech, guaranteed by the First Amendment.

Despite repeated requests for comments, the governor's Office of Public Affairs has refused to answer any questions about the incident at Western State until it is thoroughly investigated. A special task force was convened October 12.

GLEN JENCKS, CALHOUN COUNTY COURT JUDGE: This court is now in session. Ladies and gentlemen of the jury, you have been sworn to try the disputed issues of fact in today's case. After you hear the evidence presented, I will instruct you on how to apply the law to reach a verdict. You are to consider only the facts presented before you in this courtroom. If you have read or heard anything about this case, you are to try to put that out of your mind. The only facts you can consider are those you find credible from the testimony and exhibits presented today. You are not to discuss the testimony with anyone during the trial. I ask that you keep an open mind until you have heard all testimony, the attorneys' closing arguments, and my instructions on the law.

The issue in this case is whether the plaintiff was libeled. As you listen to the presentations and testimony, bear in mind that to prove a public official or public figure was libeled, the disputed publication must be shown to have been: 1) false, 2) defamatory, and 3) published with a reckless disregard for the truth or the falsity of its contents. Before you adjourn to deliberate, I will review these three requirements and what they mean.

I do want to remind you to treat each witness called in this case equally and to believe or disbelieve them as individuals. Hold them in no less or no more esteem simply because they hold public office or are figures in the community.

If you should find that the defendant *has* libeled the plaintiff, we will hold a second trial to determine the amount of damages to be awarded.

We are now ready for counsel for the plaintiff to present his opening statement. Mr. Michaelson, you may proceed.

BRIAN MICHAELSON, ATTORNEY FOR THE PLAINTIFF: Good morning. Ladies and gentlemen of the jury, I will show you through the evidence at hand that journalist Gloria Wright defamed Governor Orville Nottingham in an article published in *The Vigilant,* a vicious rag that recalls the days of the underground press. On October 15, it contained a front-page article that purported to analyze the tragedy at Western State University. Some of the facts of that tragedy may be known to you through news accounts, but I will present a brief summary here.

A small group of students at Western State University organized a protest against U.S. policies concerning South Africa. In contrast to many of the protests that have occurred on this topic throughout the country, the one at Western boded the threat of violence. A student group called the Alliance for the Oppressed, which many students characterize as a violent fringe element, was involved in the planning of this protest. The Alliance spoke openly of using violence to get its point across.

Because of such talk and the very real possibility of violence, Governor Nottingham ordered a small detachment of the National Guard to Whittier, home of Western State. The Guard was told to protect the citizens of Whittier and to protect the students at Western State—both those who were demonstrating and those who were not.

Tragically, despite the governor's precautions, violence did erupt during the rally. Two young people died. A full investigation into the incident continues at this time.

The tragedy at Western naturally occasioned great controversy, both in talk among the citizens of this state and in articles published in the press. While some have criticized the governor for his actions, one publication, *The Vigilant,* accused the governor of complicity in the deaths of the two students.

I will show this accusation is false, impugning the governor's good name. I will further show that *The Vigilant* could easily have seen that the governor acted only in the state's best interests and cannot be accused of contributing to the tragic events at Western State. In essence, *The Vigilant* maliciously libeled the governor.

Thank you, ladies and gentlemen of the jury, for allowing me to present this overview of the governor's case.

JUDGE JENCKS: Ms. King, do you have any opening remarks to make at this time?

SHIRLEY KING, COUNSEL FOR THE DEFENDANT: Yes, I do, your honor. Ladies and gentlemen of the jury, it is a sad occasion that brings me before you today. Sad in that this whole affair arises from the deaths of two young people. Patricia Renicke, Frank Waldman and their fellow demonstrators were engaged in an activity that the Founding Fathers fought for the right to have: that is the right to peaceable political protest, as guaranteed by the First Amendment to the U.S. Constitution.

The students were exercising their responsibilities as citizens to make those in authority aware of their views. In this instance, they wanted an end to the commitment of state university funds to corporations that invest in the apartheid power structure of South Africa. They believed that since Western State University is funded in part by the taxes of citizens of this state and by the tuition they pay, you and I, as well as the students, subsidize the interests of the ruling class in South Africa when the university invests in American companies that do business there.

Just as the students at Western were exercising their First Amendment rights as citizens of this state, Ms. Wright was exercising her First Amendment freedoms as a member of the press. The First Amendment of the United States Constitution specifically protects the freedom of the press. The Founding Fathers wrote that protection into the law of this land because they realized how crucial that freedom was to an open, democratic society. The press checks the misuse or abuse of governmental power by exposing it to the populace.

In investigating and writing her article on the occurences at Western State, Gloria Wright represented each of us. We will show that she carried on the highest journalistic traditions in her careful investigation of the events leading to the tragedy. She took no liberties, but merely wrote the truth. For this, she should be rewarded, not punished.

JUDGE JENCKS: Very well. Counselor Michaelson, you are now free to call your first witness.

MICHAELSON: Counsel for the plantiff calls Governor Orville Nottingham to the stand. *(The governor is sworn in.)* Please state your name and occupation for the court.

GOVERNOR ORVILLE NOTTINGHAM: I am Orville Nottingham, governor of this great state.

MICHAELSON: How long have you served as governor and what kinds of duties does the job entail?

NOTTINGHAM: The people, last year, were good enough to elect me to my fourth four-year term as governor. The job of governor is a difficult one, determining policies for economic growth, the general welfare, health and safety of the citizenry, and the betterment of our lives. I would like to think that the great support I have received from the public indicates that I have done a good job in fulfilling these enormous responsibilities.

MICHAELSON: Governor, I would like to draw your attention to the events at Western State University on October 10. Could you please tell us what advance knowledge you had of the demonstration at Western State University?

NOTTINGHAM: Certainly. Let me tell you first that I have had experience with campus riots before. Depending on the character of any demonstration, local or state authorities have to station security forces around the scene to stave off possible problems. That means we've got to know as much as we can about these things beforehand in order to deal with them in the most knowledgeable way. We want our men to know the issues involved, what groups and how many individuals are participating, and where to concentrate their forces so they don't arrive on the scene too late to control what's happening.

This procedure was followed in the October demonstration at Western State University. When planning for protests began there, we soon discovered radical groups were at work: groups that talked of making bombs, of taking over the university. Obviously, we were concerned about the implicit danger their plans posed for state property and for other students. In addition, university and Whittier officials had often complained about shortages in security manpower in the past, so my office wanted to make sure they could handle what might turn out to be a violent protest.

After getting a full report on the situation at Western State, I decided sending in the National Guard was our best bet to avoid a full-scale riot. After all, the Guard is trained in the best tactics to handle such situations. They were the perfect plug for the lack of security manpower at Western State.

MICHAELSON: Despite this precaution, governor, why did the demonstration at Western State end in the deaths of two students?

NOTTINGHAM: Unfortunately, even the best-laid plans sometimes go awry. While we took every precaution we could think of, the actions of groups like Alliance for the Oppressed made a peaceful protest impossible to attain. I believe that, given the circumstances, we should be thankful the violence was no worse than what it was.

I am sorry that Patricia Renicke and Frank Waldman happened to be in the wrong place at the wrong time. I extend my sympathies to their parents.

MICHAELSON: Using hindsight, something that in the heat of decision you did not have, would you have done anything differently?

NOTTINGHAM: No. Well, we might have added sound trucks or some other means to warn students about the danger of violence.

MICHAELSON: I hand you a document marked Plaintiff's Exhibit A. Do you recognize it?

NOTTINGHAM: Yes, this is the defamatory article that accused me of killing those poor students. Nothing could be further from the truth.

MICHAELSON: Let the record show that this is the article "Two-fold Tragedy Tears Campus" in the October 15 edition of *The Vigilant*. Would you read to the court the portion of the article that prompted you to bring this lawsuit?

NOTTINGHAM: The lie they published says, and this is the quotation, "the tragic shooting of two student protesters at Western State University earlier this week was the natural consequence of orders issued by Governor Orville Nottingham." It continued, "When he called out the National Guard to Western State to contain the students' anti-apartheid demonstration, Nottingham set up the scenario that led directly to the students' deaths." It makes those accusations despite the well-reported fact that I sent the Guard to deter violence.

MICHAELSON: Thank you, governor. No further questions.

KING: Governor Nottingham, a number of years ago you came into office on a law-and-order campaign. In your campaign rhetoric, you said the state and the nation had to rise out of what you called "the mire of the 1960s," which you described as "an era of unrestrained lawlessness' and "violence trying to pass itself off as civil disobedience."

Talking about the campus activists of those days, you said some of them were "just kids with nothing to do who wanted to create a commotion." How would you characterize the demonstrators at Western State? Were they throwbacks to the protestors you opposed in the Sixties?

NOTTINGHAM: I have never opposed the right to peaceful demonstrations as guaranteed by the First Amendment. And I have never been unfriendly to such demonstrations or to anyone's First Amendment rights. However, I don't approve of students who would tear down the very state that supports them. Many of those students wouldn't be at Western State at all but for grants and subsidies from the government.

In the end, I think that anyone who cares to look at what happened at Western would come to the same conclusion I have—there are a lot of ominous similarities between what happened there in October and the riots of the '60s. I sent the Guard there to prevent violence.

KING: Governor, do you think your belief that this would be a 1960's-style demonstration could have influenced the way the National Guard perceived the situation at Western State?

NOTTINGHAM: I instructed the Guard to go into Whittier prepared to protect both the citizens and the students. That was all.

KING: Governor Nottingham, didn't you instruct the Guard to give the protesters, and I quote, "a good spanking"?

NOTTINGHAM: Those words have been taken out of context. I meant that those protesters who wantonly destroyed government or state property should be duly punished...under the law. Nothing more.

KING: Governor, were you aware what issue the students were protesting at Western State on October 10?

NOTTINGHAM: Yes, the students were protesting against the university's investment in companies that do business in South Africa.

KING: What didn't the students like about those investments?

MICHAELSON: Objection. This is not a political forum. The information is immaterial.

KING: Your honor, the information is material. It goes to the motivation for the plaintiff's actions.

JENCKS: Objection overruled.

KING: The question was: What were the students' objections to that investment.

NOTTINGHAM: They claimed those investments support the South African government's policy of apartheid, which makes racial separation the law.

KING: Governor, would the students have characterized that system of government in stronger language? That is, would apartheid be outlawed in America as racist and discriminatory?

NOTTINGHAM: I suppose that would have been the interpretation of the more radical elements on campus.

KING: Governor, do you personally have investments in South Africa?

NOTTINGHAM: Yes, I do. It is a matter of public record.

KING: Do you have any qualms about continuing those investments?

NOTTINGHAM: No. When the moral issue is unclear as in this case, I say it's good business to go with the most lucrative financial route. At this point, I support the board of trustees' decision to keep university money where it will produce. What stock the state university system has in South Africa is invested with blue-chip companies that give us good returns on our investments. I think we should continue along that path until we are shown — conclusively — that we should do otherwise. We should not get ourselves involved in another country's politics.

KING: Did you feel personally attacked by the student protest at Western State?

NOTTINGHAM: I tried to remain a neutral judge of the situation there, but I would be less than candid if I said being hung in effigy and having expletives flung at me didn't anger me.

KING: Thank you, governor. No further questions.

JUDGE JENCKS: Counsel, call your next witness.

MICHAELSON: Counsel for the plaintiff now calls Garrison Kiley. *(Kiley is sworn in.)* Please state your name and occupation for the record.

GARRISON KILEY: I am Garrison Kiley, a member of the governor's security force and a captain in the National Guard unit called to Western State last October.

MICHAELSON: Captain Kiley, how would you describe the atmosphere when your unit arrived in Whittier the day of the demonstration?

KILEY: Well, it was tense. We wouldn't have been called in if it hadn't been.

MICHAELSON: Captain Kiley, what did you expect when you got to Western? How had you been briefed beforehand?

KILEY: We had intelligence showing that radical factions had infiltrated the student groups organizing the demonstration. These radical groups, chief among them the Alliance for the Oppressed, had vowed to use violence instead of peaceful protest to make a symbolic statement.

MICHAELSON: What happened after you were on campus?

KILEY: When we got there, we were told to concentrate most of our forces around the administration building. The demonstration was planned for the mall in front of it. As we marched to the administration building, we could see lots of students around. When we got closer, we heard lots of shouting but I couldn't really make out much of it. Some black members of the Guard told me that protesters were taunting them and saying they were Uncle Toms who would sell their brothers down the river.

MICHAELSON: Can you tell us what started the violence that led to the deaths of Western students Patricia Renicke and Frank Waldman?

KILEY: I don't think we'll ever know exactly: Emotions had made the situation a real tinderbox. In the close quarters we were in, the students outnumbered us. Even crack troops like the National Guard couldn't contain the crowd. It just became a mob scene. A free-for-all.

MICHAELSON: Was there anything you could have done at this point to prevent the violence?

KILEY: No, it simply had gotten out of hand. I think it would have been worse — more students injured and damage to property — if the Guard had not been posted. We heard that the bombs we expected were not used because of the presence of the Guard.

KING: Objection. That last statement was hearsay.

JENCKS: Objection sustained. Strike Mr. Kiley's last sentence from the record. Jurors, you are to ignore the testimony about the bombs.

MICHAELSON: Thank you, Captain Kiley. Your witness.

KING: Captain Kiley, you've assessed what happened at Western as the unavoidable result of a mob gone out of control. Is that correct?

KILEY: Yes, it is.

KING: You've stated that your briefing warned you of possible violence by radical groups. Who gave you this briefing?

KILEY: Warren Spellman, director of the governor's security force.

KING: Did you receive an additional briefing from the governor.

KILEY: Yes.

KING: What did the governor say?

KILEY: He told us our job was to prevent violence and that we were the experts in deciding how best to do it.

KING: Did he tell you to "give those kids a good spanking?"

KILEY: I don't recall his exact words. He did indicate that the troublemakers should be punished.

KING: And who were identified as the troublemakers?

KILEY: The radicals.

KING: Captain Kiley, could a Guardsmen who was angered by the protesters have interpreted the governor's remark as a go-ahead for more decisive actions against the demonstrators? Could that remark have made it more acceptable to use physical force to silence the protest?

KILEY: I can't speculate on that.

KING: But that might have been a reasonable interpretation?

KILEY: I suppose someone could have thought so.

KING: No further questions, Captain.

MICHAELSON: The plaintiff calls Janice Eberhardt. *(Eberhardt is sworn in.)* Please state your name and occupation for the record.

JANICE EBERHARDT: My name is Janice Eberhardt. I am a student at Western State University.

MICHAELSON: What connection did you have to the demonstration that took place at the university on October 10?

EBERHARDT: Well, I am a former member of the Alliance for the Oppressed *because* of what happened October 10. It's because of them that two friends of mine are dead.

MICHAELSON: Could you explain just how the Alliance precipitated the violence at Western?

EBERHARDT: The Alliance had been in on the demonstration from the beginning. Some of our members were agitating other student groups to make a symbolic "statement." They talked about the need to make a physical statement with some impact, maybe even throwing garbage or blood on anyone who tried to stop or monitor the protest. If we didn't do something like that, they said, people would think campus activism today is a sell-out, run by a bunch of namby-pamby little kids too scared to take a chance. They were trying to mesmerize everyone with mythology from the Sixties.

MICHAELSON: What sort of response was the Alliance getting from the students? Were people interested in what they had to say?

EBERHARDT: At first, the Alliance fringe didn't seem to be able to convince the more mainstream groups that "their" way was the way to go. But those who sided with Alliance were very vocal about what they thought should be done. As the date for the demonstration neared, no one quite knew exactly what role they would take.

On the afternoon planned for the demonstration, the tenth, I was down by the administration building when the protest was set to start. Most of the outspoken members of Alliance were there, looking edgy. I was worried about what they had going. Suddenly, we saw what looked like an army advancing from beyond the administration building.

People started shouting that the governor had called out the National Guard to shut us up. People were screaming, "It's just like Kent State," and "They're going to shoot." I think all the shouting was from the Alliance members, trying to stir up the crowd. Many of the students who had planned only peaceful protest seemed to think the Alliance was vindicated by this confrontation with the military. The Alliance said if we continued to ignore this and act like sheep, we would soon be subjugated just like the blacks in South Africa.

There *wasn't* time to really think about what they were saying. Or at least no one seemed to. The loudest shouters called for total anarchy, and confusion reigned. Some Alliance members started throwing rocks and bottles at the Guard. Then the shots rang out.

MICHAELSON: Ms. Eberhardt, did the students really plan a peaceful protest?

EBERHARDT: No. I don't think they knew what they were doing. They were misguided and inadvertently led to the violence that killed Patty Renicke and Frank Waldman. People got too caught up in the glamour of protesting. There's a way to work within the system and get things done. We don't have to tear society end from end in order to change things. If we had used a different method, maybe Patty and Frank would be alive today.

MICHAELSON: Thank you, Ms. Eberhardt. Your witness.

KING: Ms. Eberhardt, the scene at the administration building that day was quite frightening, wasn't it?

EBERHARDT: It was terrible. Everyone was pushing and shouting. We were caught up in some awful, angry roar.

KING: What was the temper of the protest like *before* the demonstrators saw the National Guard advancing? Had it been peaceful up until that point?

EBERHARDT: There had been no violence until then, but some members of Alliance were out there calling for drastic action,...for violence.

KING: Ms. Eberhardt, were the students listening to the members of the Alliance then?

EBERHARDT: I don't think so. They had their own speakers and agenda. But I think the Alliance would have continued to escalate the protest until they were the center of it.

KING: Very well, Ms. Eberhardt. No further questions.

JENCKS: The plaintiff may call its next witness.

MICHAELSON: I would like to call Gloria Wright to the witness stand. *(Ms. Wright is sworn in at the witness stand. Counselor Michaelson moves in to question her, handing her a document as he does so.)* Please state your name and occupation for the record.

WRIGHT: My name is Gloria Wright. I am a reporter for *The Vigilant,* a weekly newspaper.

MICHAELSON: Ms. Wright, you are the author of this article, which was marked Plaintiff's Exhibit A. Isn't that so?

WRIGHT: Yes.

MICHAELSON: Ms. Wright, have you ever met Governor Nottingham before this trial?

WRIGHT: No.

MICHAELSON: Have you ever covered him as a journalist or worked in a political campaign for one of his opponents?

WRIGHT: No.

MICHAELSON: But you were a press aide in the campaign of a candidate for the state legislature, who ran on an anti-Nottingham platform. Isn't that so?

WRIGHT: Yes, that's true.

MICHAELSON: Is it fair to say that you generally oppose the governor's policies?

WRIGHT: Yes.

MICHAELSON: Did this affect the way you wrote your story?

WRIGHT: I described the governor factually after uncovering all his actions leading to the Western State demonstration. He acted out of a fundamental political disagreement with the demonstrators, not reasoned policy. Calling out the Guard was Nottingham's way to silence what he didn't want to hear.

The governor's actions led directly to the tragedy that took the lives of two young students. While Nottingham did not wield any weapons, he is at least partly to blame for the deaths of Patricia Renicke and Frank Waldman.

MICHAELSON: Is that undisputed fact, Ms. Wright, or is your feeling about what happened at Western mere intuition, an opinion?

WRIGHT: If you read further in the article, my interviews and investigations bear the truth of those accusations out. If the official investigation isn't hamstrung by the governor, it will discover the same things.

MICHAELSON: Ms. Wright, let me rephrase my question. Was your article in *The Vigilant* a news story or an editorial?

WRIGHT: It was run as a news story.

MICHAELSON: Now, a news story is supposed to stick to the facts. Where are the specific facts that led your story to accuse Governor Nottingham of the crime of murder?

WRIGHT: He told the National Guard that there would be violence, when he should have known that violence was unlikely to occur. He gave them the green light to punish the protesters. He should have known the Guard's presence would incite the few agitators in the crowd who otherwise would have lacked a target for their violence.

I am not saying he knowingly sent the Guard to the campus to murder the students. I am saying his actions exhibited a reckless disregard for the likely consequences of his orders.

MICHAELSON: Ms. Wright, what political classification would you give your newspaper?

WRIGHT: I don't like to put anything in a cut-and-dried category. I suppose if I *had* to characterize *The Vigilant* in some way I would say it is progressive.

MICHAELSON: Ms. Wright, could "progressive" be a euphemism for what most Americans would think of as left wing, and some would even call radical?

WRIGHT: I suppose it could in some cases.

MICHAELSON: Ms. Wright, would you say that the principal witnesses you quoted in your article would be opposed to Governor Nottingham politically?

WRIGHT: I interviewed many of the same people you have called as witnesses, counselor. It's just that the two of us have put a different slant on the information we gathered. It's true that many of the people I interviewed for my story aren't necessarily enamoured with the governor's way of doing business. But that doesn't mean what they told me is not more accurate than the official line put out by the governor's office. Besides, I did interview some people who could be said to be supporters of the governor. What they claimed had happened just wasn't substantiated by the facts. In addition, I gave the governor a chance to respond to the charges that were to appear in the article and he declined my request.

MICHAELSON: But, Ms. Wright, isn't it true that the governor declined that request because the incident was still under investigation?

WRIGHT: That was the response his press office gave, but some of the questions raised at Western could have been answered before the inquiry was finished. The investigation is just a stalling tactic.

MICHAELSON: Is that your opinion, Ms. Wright? Aren't such views usually labeled as "analysis" or "editorial comment"?

WRIGHT: Officially, the investigation isn't over. I predict it will continue just until the heat cools on the governor. Then, an announcement can be made without inflaming more passions.

MICHAELSON: Your witness, counselor.

KING: Your honor, I do not wish to question my client at this time. I do reserve the right to recall her for later questioning.

JENCKS: Does the counsel for the plaintiff have any more witnesses to call?

MICHAELSON: No, your honor. Counsel for the plaintiff rests its case.

JENCKS: The court now gives the defendant leave to present her case and call her own witnesses.

KING: Thank you, your honor, I would now like to call Jeremy Bentham. *(Jeremy Bentham is sworn in.)* For the record, please state your name and occupation.

JEREMY BENTHAM: My name is Jeremy Bentham. I'm a student at Western State University. I helped organize the demonstration.

KING: Mr. Bentham, could you tell us why and how the demonstration was organized?

BENTHAM: A number of different student groups, all of whom were opposed to university funds supporting corporations with outlets in South Africa, met in late September to organize some type of political protest. We had been doing mailings and putting up posters, but we wanted to do something that would make more of a statement. Since Western State starts its term at the end of August, we had already gauged the amount of support we could count on from the student body. We felt that support was pretty concrete as we sat down to plan out a rally.

The protest was planned by a range of student groups that fell all along the philosophical and ideological spectrum. Of course, there were some present who could be classified as radical. They might have been a bit unhappy with the more moderate approach the more established and mainstream student groups wanted to take. But, to my way of thinking, eventually their rhetoric cooled and they agreed to stand with the group so that we could present a united front.

KING: Although almost everyone had agreed to work toward a unified protest, could there have been stalwarts who secretly continued to plan a more radical, a more violent, alternative?

BENTHAM: If there were, as the governor and the university administration has implied, I was unaware of it. Even in the remote possibility that some were thinking along those lines, I still think the university administration and the government overreacted to the threat. Pressure from their peers, the huge majority that wanted a peaceful demonstration, would have blunted any talk of violence from the isolated few who might still have advocated it.

KING: Mr. Bentham, with the protest underway, what effect did the presence of the National Guard have on the demonstrators?

BENTHAM: Seeing the National Guard advancing from beyond the administration building inflamed everyone's emotions. People were scared, but people were angry first. It seemed as if the university and government administration were trying to silence any political opposition: like an iron boot in the face. The governor's reaction made it an "us" and "them" situation: the Sixties all over again. When university and government officials overreacted like that, it gave credence to the more radical perspective of groups like the Alliance for the Oppressed.

KING: Mr. Bentham, would you say that the actions of the Guard were directed at any specific protesters? We have heard testimony here today that suggests the Guard was particularly concerned about, and indeed had "intelligence" on, radical groups like Alliance for the Oppressed. Did they seem to single out anyone in particular?

BENTHAM: No, not that I could tell. It was just that certain people were in the wrong place at the wrong time. Patty Renicke wasn't affiliated with any of those groups, but she did have friends scattered among them. That was why she had been particularly valuable in planning the rally: she could carry on a dialogue with just about anyone. Her death is a tragic irony.

KING: Thank you, Mr. Bentham.

JUDGE JENCKS: The plaintiff may now cross-examine the witness.

MICHAELSON: Could it be, Mr. Bentham, that the students are blaming the National Guard after-the-fact in this manner so that they don't have to face their own guilt?

BENTHAM: No. I don't believe that is true.

MICHAELSON: Thank you, Mr. Bentham

JUDGE JENCKS: Are there any further defense witnesses?

KING: Yes, I would like to now call the defendant, Gloria Wright, to the stand. *(Wright is sworn in.)* Ms. Wright, could you explain, in your own words, why you chose to present Governor Nottingham as you did in your article for *The Vigilant*?

WRIGHT: I drew connections between the governor and the deaths at Western because he is at least partially to blame for what happened there. It was the National Guard who fired the guns at Western State, but they wouldn't have been there in the first place if not for Governor Nottingham's paranoia over student protests. He precipitated the tragedy by sending agents to the campus, inflaming the situation with the presence of National

Guard in full combat dress, personally instructing the Guard to "spank" the students, and circulating rumors of bombs that didn't actually exist.

Governor Nottingham himself holds stock in three companies which do business in South Africa. People have a right to know he had more in mind than public safety, since ending the policies that were protested would affect his own pocketbook.

KING: What do you mean by this "paranoia" the governor has?

WRIGHT: In the past, we've seen the governor repeatedly show his disapproval of any sort of civil disobedience or demonstrations. He rode into office on a law-and-order campaign by playing on others' paranoias and fears. Sometimes I think he believes life is a John Wayne movie and it's always time to circle the wagons.

If the governor had his way, everyone would just acquiesce to the policies of the establishment, with no questions asked. He has a distorted sense of reality that makes him see his actions as governor in a weird sort of father-knows-best fashion.

Simply put, if the National Guard had not been called in, the tension at Western State University would not have been heightened to the point that violence broke out. Calling the Guard in escalated the conflict.

KING: Your witness.

MICHAELSON: I have no questions for this witness.

JUDGE JENCKS: Counsel for the defendant, do you have any more witnesses to call?

KING: No, your honor, the defense rests its case.

JUDGE JENCKS: Very well. We are now ready for counsel to present their closing arguments.

MICHAELSON: Ladies and gentlemen of the jury, your honor, testimony made here today shows Gloria Wright and her newspaper clearly libeled Governor Nottingham. Her article in *The Vigilant* meets the three tests for libel: Ms. Wright made defamatory and false statements about the governor with a completely reckless disregard for the truth.

No one questions whether Ms. Wright's article was defamatory: it is obviously so. It accuses the governor of nothing less than murder in the tragic death of two student protesters. We have shown this accusation is false. The governor, acting in the best interests of the community, ordered the National Guard to Western State for the singular duty of keeping the peace.

You heard the testimony of Garrison Kiley that the governor tried to obtain the best possible intelligence about what was planned on campus. He wanted to be prepared for every contingency, and he wanted to be certain he didn't overreact. You heard testimony that his agents did not harrass the peaceful demonstrators, but concentrated on those reputed to have bombs. You heard Janice Eberhardt, a reformed member of the radical Alliance for the Oppressed, tell us that the group was determined to bring about violence to call attention to their cause—that they were swayed by some romanticized vision of the campus bombings of the Sixties. You heard her lay the blame for the tragedy at the feet of these radicals.

You also heard Gloria Wright, author of the article, reveal her own prejudices against the governor. She has campaigned against him, she opposes his policies and she actually blames him personally for the South African apartheid policies. This is not the open mind of a fair journalist. It is instead the biased thoughts of someone with an ax to grind. Wright did not simply marshall the facts; she interpreted them through her own political prejudices. She did not try to discover how real the threat of violence was that prompted the governor to call out the Guard. This is journalistic recklessness that can only result in untruth.

The governor, a man of considerable experience and mature judgment, called out the Guard to protect the citizens of this state. We cannot expect him to be all-knowing and foresee the tragedy that occurred. On the contrary, I ask, who knows how many more would have died if the governor had not called in the Guard. Gloria Wright's article looks at the situation through a very distorted prism in its unfair attack on the governor. Jury members, I think you will agree that the integrity of a man's name is very important. Once we strip away the niceties of civilization, it is all each of us is left with.

But, far worse than the attacks on the governor's good name is that the *Vigilant* article undermines the security and safety of this state. After a tragedy such as the demonstration at Western proved to be, the best thing to do is to come together and heal our wounds. Instead, Ms. Wright rubs salt back into them. She does the state a disservice and attacks its very governance and functioning by creating this crisis in self-confidence.

Such behavior is patently unpatriotic. It sows the seeds of doubt and saps the strength of the populace and the popular will. If it is allowed to continue, we will once again find ourselves fighting the demons that reared their ugly heads in this country during the 1960s. We don't need all of that self-doubt and recrimination. It weakens this state and the whole country from within.

Since we have shown the *Vigilant* article to be false, defamatory, and published with a reckless disregard for the truth, under the law, Ms. Wright is liable for damages for the harm she caused to the good reputation of the governor. I only ask that you, the jury, do your duty.

JUDGE JENCKS: Counsel for the defendant may now present her closing argument.

KING: Thank you, your honor. Ladies and gentlemen of the jury, I think after a little reflection you will note that the story written by Gloria Wright has received the same condescending attitude as did all of the demonstrators at Western. At best, they were treated as young, naive innocents who were not even dry behind the ears. In this way, their arguments, however relevant to public policy concerns, were relegated to ridicule or anonymity. At worst, the demonstrators and Gloria Wright are seen as radical subversives who should be "spanked," or their arguments snuffed out.

I suggest to the jury that accepting only the "established," official way of believing, of thinking, of acting runs counter to our history and culture. Such a course is, in fact, very dangerous: therein lies peril—the peril of autocratic governments that impose an official creed, that excise all vestiges of individuality or of personality from life.

The beauty of the political system we have set up in this country is that it allows for a variance in opinion; in fact, out of the sifting of philosophies and viewpoints we may arrive at truths for our times. We do ourselves a disservice by ignoring the novel or the untried and by only respecting the orthodox. Such an approach limits us by negating new, different, and invigorating ways of looking at things.

We must be careful to insure a voice not only for those who have gained political power, by virtue of their mature age or reason, but for those who fall outside of the political process. If we don't do this, we lose out on fresh perspectives that would enliven our society and risk becoming an ossified dinosaur.

The governor's action at Western State showed his overwhelming concern for the status quo and a lack of appreciation for different perspectives. It could very well be interpreted as a measure to silence the students' criticism of policies he so vehemently supports. In a way, the governor violated the students' rights to peaceably assemble, as guaranteed by the Constitution of this country.

But the rights of the students or the correct policy to be adopted toward South Africa is not the issue before us today. What we are here to decide is whether the defendant, journalist Gloria Wright, libeled the governor in her article about the rally at Western.

I think after hearing the testimony here today you will agree this article gives a needed perspective to the public debate and asks questions that need to be answered. I don't think we'll have all those answers even when the investigation into the incident is complete. The "truth" of what happened at Western will be more difficult to ferret out than that. The "truth" of what happened at Western State, the "correct" policy toward South Africa, are both matters that are open to debate, debates of ethics and of policy considerations. And, that is how such questions must be handled—through debate and discussion in the public arena.

Through this civil action against Gloria Wright, the governor has found an effective device to stifle criticism. However, the First Amendment was written to guarantee a free and robust press that questioned precisely those actions of government that government would not want openly questioned. In this regard, Gloria Wright was carrying on the best journalistic traditions. No public official should be free from the scrutiny of the press. It is not the press that makes judgments, however. It is the public. And, that public has a right to know all facts and hear all viewpoints before it reaches a conclusion.

This freedom to comment on our government, and to criticize when necessary, gives us a check on its unbridled power. Only through such constructive criticism have we been able to uncover cancers like Watergate and similar violations of the public trust.

The right of Ms. Wright to publish critical articles has been upheld by the Supreme Court. When it comes to criticizing the actions of public officials, the Supreme Court recognized the necessity for the press to be fairly free of any fetters long ago. In 1964, the celebrated case of *New York Times v. Sullivan* set the standards we still must abide by today. The majority opinion in that case declared that debate on public issues should be "uninhibited, robust, and wide open." It went on to say such debate could include "vehement" and "caustic" attacks on government and public officials.

Gloria Wright did not libel Governor Nottingham. The governor has failed to prove the *Vigilant* article false. In your verdict, you have a chance to stand up for the very best in American traditions: that the liberty of the press shall not fall victim to the arbitrary power of government and those who would cover up their mistakes if we did not have a free press. By finding the defendant not liable, you will have stood up for the principle of speaking and writing truth.

Thank you.

JENCKS: Members of the jury, now that you have heard all of the evidence and the argument of counsel, it becomes my duty to give you the instructions of the court concerning the law applicable to this case.

It is your duty as jurors to follow the law as I shall state it to you, and to apply that law to the facts as you find them from the evidence in the case. You are not to single out one instruction alone as stating the law, but must consider the instructions as a whole. Neither are you to be concerned with the wisdom of any rule of law stated by me.

Your verdict must represent the considered judgment of each juror. In order to return a verdict, it is necessary that each juror agree. In other words, your verdict must be unanimous.

It is your duty as jurors to consult with one another and to deliberate with a view to reaching an agreement, if you can do so without violence to individual judgment. Each of you must decide the case for yourself, but only after an impartial consideration of all the evidence in the case with your fellow jurors. In the course of your deliberations, do not hesitate to re-examine your own views and change your opinion, if convinced it is erroneous. But do not surrender your honest conviction as to the weight or effect of the evidence, solely because of the opinion of your fellow jurors, or for the mere purpose of returning a verdict.

Remember at all times you are not partisans. You are judges—judges of the facts. Your sole interest is to seek the truth from the evidence in the case.

Now, I have said that you must consider all of the evidence. This does not mean, however, that you must accept all of the evidence as true or accurate.

You are the sole judges of the credibility or "believability" of each witness. You should consider his or her relationship to the plaintiff or to the defendant; his candor, fairness and intelligence; and the extent to which he has been supported or contradicted by other credible evidence. You may, in short, accept or reject the testimony of any witness in whole or in part.

Also, the weight of the evidence is not necessarily determined by the number of witnesses testifying as to the existence or non-existence of any fact. You may find that the testimony of a smaller number of witnesses about any fact is more credible than the testimony of a larger number of witnesses to the contrary.

This is a case of libel. A libel is a false and malicious defamation of a person by printing or writing, tending to provoke him to wrath or to expose him to public hatred, contempt or ridicule, or to deprive him of the benefits of public confidence and social intercourse.

Under our law a person's good reputation is held in high regard, and when it is falsely attacked the law gives him the opportunity to bring a libel action to recover damages. When the plaintiff is a public official, and the alleged libel relates to his conduct in or fitness for office, then the plaintiff must bear an additional requirement and must establish by clear and convincing evidence that the alleged libel was published with actual malice.

To find for the plaintiff, each of the following must have been proven to your satisfaction:

- First, that the defendant published written statements as opposed to oral statements;
- Second, that the written statements constituted libel as that term was defined for you in these instructions;
- Third, that the publication was "of and concerning the plaintiff;"
- Fourth, that the publication was communicated to third persons;
- Fifth, that the publication was false in some material particular; and
- Sixth, that the written statements were published with actual malice.

The burden is on the plaintiff to prove the first five of these elements by a "preponderance of the evidence." A preponderance of the evidence means evidence which, when considered and compared with that opposed to it, has more convincing force and produces in your minds a belief that what counsel seeks to prove is more likely true than not true. In other words, to establish a claim by a "preponderance of the evidence" merely means to prove that the claim is more likely so than it is not so.

In determining whether any fact in issue has been proved by a preponderance of the evidence, the jury may consider the testimony of all the witnesses, regardless of who may have called them, and all the exhibits received in evidence, regardless of who may have produced them. If the proof should fail to establish any essential element of the plaintiff's claim by a preponderance of the evidence, the jury should find for the defendant.

The burden of proof becomes stricter with regard to the sixth element: that of actual malice. The plaintiff has the burden of establishing by clear and convincing evidence that the publication was made with actual malice. Clear and convincing evidence commands a higher degree of proof than a preponderance of the evidence. It means you must have a firm belief in the validity of the evidence.

A publication is made with "actual malice," as that term is used in this charge, if it is made with knowledge that it is false, or with reckless disregard of whether it is false or not. For the defendant to have acted recklessly, the plaintiff must prove that the defendant had a high degree of awareness of the probable falsity of the statements when published.

If you find that the plaintiff has established these six elements you may find for the plaintiff. If you find that he has failed to establish any one of the elements, then it is your duty to find for the defendant.

Memorandum on Legal Issues
Libel

The law of defamation tries to balance two sometimes competing interests in American society: the societal interest in freedom of expression and individual interests in reputation, both of a personal and proprietary nature.

Defamation is defined as statements that tend to harm the reputation of a person and to lower him in the estimation of the community or to deter third persons from associating with him. *Steaks Unlimited, Inc. v. Deaner,* 623 F.2d 264, 267 (3d Cir. 1980). Damage to reputation can be in reference to one's business or profession; within a small, but significant, segment of the community; or through imputations of unsavory characteristics like insanity or poverty. Spoken defamation is referred to as slander, and written defamation, libel. To constitute libel, the defamation must be "published," that is, it must be perceived by someone other than the person defamed. Courts have ruled that defamatory radio and television broadcasts qualify as libel.

Throughout most of American history, the common law of each state governed defamation. These laws usually placed a high premium on an individual's right to reputation, recognizing its importance to each person's sense of human dignity and self worth.

Coexisting with this common law formulation of defamation law, the First Amendment to the U.S. Constitution incorporated the belief that people must be able to comment on, and criticize, government and its officials. Only through open debate on matters of public concern, the framers believed, would just and honest government be insured. Initially, First Amendment guarantees were binding on only the national government, but many state constitutions contained clauses designed to protect freedom of expression. In *Near v. Minnesota,* 283 U.S. 697 (1931), the Supreme Court declared the First Amendment applicable to state action as well. Chief Justice Charles Evans Hughes declared for the Court majority, "It is no longer open to doubt that the liberty of the press, and of speech, is within the liberty safeguarded by the due process clause of the Fourteenth Amendment from invasion by state action." *Id.* at 707.

In the *Near* ruling, the Court explicitly recognized the importance of free speech and a free press to the American system and outlawed prior restraints on publications in all but extreme circumstances. The Court also stated:

> The fact that the liberty of the press may be abused by miscreant purveyors of scandal does not make any the less necessary the immunity of the press from previous restraint in dealing with official misconduct. Subsequent punishment for such abuses as may exist is the appropriate remedy, consistent with constitutional privilege.
>
> Id. at 720.

Although the Court could not condone censorship in all but emergency situations, it allowed for after-the-fact punishment of libelous publications. In *Near* and later cases, the Court noted that certain forms of expression, including libel, enjoy no constitutional protection. See *Chaplinsky v. New Hampshire,* 315 U.S. 568, 572 (1942).

Libel and Constitutional Protections

In 1964, the Supreme Court made the First Amendment applicable to libel law in *New York Times v. Sullivan,* 376 U.S. 254 (1964). *Sullivan* imposed a constitutional and national standard on libel actions involving public officials and outlined a three-part test for plaintiffs to meet to recover civil damages. To be judged libelous and actionable for damages, the publication in question had to be 1) false, 2) defamatory and 3) published with reckless disregard for the truth—or actual malice.

Progeny of *Sullivan* further nationalized the law of libel and slander. Lawsuits brought by a "public figure" became subject to constitutional scrutiny. *Curtis Publishing Company v. Butts,* 388 U.S. 130 (1966). Four years later, a plurality of the Court tried to divide libel actions into two categories, determined on the basis of plaintiffs' involvement in an event of public interest and not on their individual status. *Rosenbloom v. Metromedia, Inc.,* 403 U.S. 29 (1970). Then in *Gertz v. Robert Welch, Inc.,* 418 U.S. 323 (1974), the Court returned to distinctions based on individuals' "public" or "private" status and set a more exacting standard for finding an individual a "public" figure. But in *Dun & Bradstreet v. Greenmoss Builders,* 53 U.S.L.W. 4866 (1985), the Court resurrected the *Rosenbloom* distinction based on the public or private nature of events associated with an alleged libel, instead of on the status of its participants.

Sullivan originated during the racially polarized climate of the 1960s and gave journalists wide latitude in reporting about public officials involved in public business. Justice William Brennan, writing for the majority, recognized its special context, stating, "we consider this case against the background of a profound national commitment to the principle that debate on public issues should be uninhibited, robust and wide-open, and that it may well include caustic and sometimes unpleasantly sharp attacks on public officials." 376 U.S. at 270.

The libel lawsuit in *Sullivan* started with a full-page March 29, 1960, *New York Times* advertisement that solicited donations to finance the civil rights movement and legal defense for the Rev. Martin Luther King Jr.

In describing the civil rights movement, the advertisement declared:

> As the whole world knows by now, thousands of Southern Negro students are engaged in widespread non-violent demonstrations in positive affirmation of the right to live in human dignity as guaranteed by the United States Constitution and the Bill of Rights. In their efforts to uphold these guarantees, they are being met by an unprecedented wave of terror by those who would deny and negate that document which the whole world looks upon as setting the pattern for modern freedom.... The Southern violators of the Constitution fear this new, non-violent brand of freedom fighter.

The advertisement, though implicating no one by name, then equated these "Southern violators" with those who bombed King's home, with those who allegedly assaulted him outside of a courtroom — and with those responsible for his previous and present arrests. Montgomery (Ala.) city commissioner L. B. Sullivan filed a libel action, charging that the advertisement contained factual errors that defamed him in his duties as supervisor of police.

The *Times* advertisement did contain a number of minor errors (officials arrested the younger Rev. King four times, not seven; demonstrators sang "The Star-Spangled Banner," not "My Country 'Tis of Thee") that made it libelous under Alabama common law. State courts rejected the reasoning put forth by the *Times* defense counsel, who asserted the advertisement was protected by the First Amendment as applied to the states through the Fourteenth Amendment. On the contrary, according to the state courts, the Fourteenth Amendment could not be used to invoke First Amendment rights, since the parties in the proceedings were not states but private litigants in a civil dispute. In addition, the state courts declared the advertisement was "commercial" speech, which does not enjoy the same constitutional protection as speech that deals with public issues.

The U.S. Supreme Court rejected the reasoning of the Alabama courts. The Court first dispensed with the plantiff's claim that the advertisement was ineligible for constitutional protection as commercial speech. On the contrary, the *Sullivan* Court declared, "it communicated information, expressed opinion, recited grievances, protested claimed abuses and sought financial support on behalf of a movement whose existence and objectives are matters of the highest public concern... Any other conclusion would discourage newspapers from carrying 'editorial advertisements' of this type and so might shut off an important outlet for the promulgation of information and ideas by persons who do not themselves have access to publishing facilities — who wish to exercise their freedom of speech even though they are not members of the press." 376 U.S. at 266.

The Court then found the strict libel rule operating in Alabama to be unconstitutional, since it presumed a statement was defamatory on its face unless a defendant proved it true. Justice Brennan wrote:

> The state rule of law is not saved by its allowance of the defense of truth. A defense for erroneous statements honestly made is no less essential here than was the requirement of proof of guilty knowledge, which, in *Smith v. California* 361 U.S. 147 (1959), we held indispensable to a valid conviction of a bookseller for possessing obscene writings for sale.
> *Id.* at 278-279.

According to Brennan, a common law statute like Alabama's would force the press, and other prospective defendants, to censor itself. "Whether or not a newspaper can survive a succession of such judgments, the pall of fear and timidity imposed upon those who would give voice to public criticism is an atmosphere in which the First Amendment freedoms cannot survive," the Court said, adding that it struck down the Alabama law because its "allowance of the defense of truth, with the burden of proving it on the defendant, does not mean that only false speech would be deferred." *Id.*

Then Brennan outlined the three-tiered standard that made defamation of public officials subject to constitutional scrutiny:

> The constitutional guarantees require, we think, a federal rule that prohibits a public official from recovering damages for a defamatory falsehood relating to his official conduct unless he proves that the statement was made with actual malice, that is, with knowledge that it was false or with reckless disregard that it was false or not.
> *Id.* at 279-280.

After *Sullivan*

A publication is not saved from a libel judgment when "true statements are interspersed in a defamatory publication otherwise false.... Moreover, the fact that a statement is literally true, as that a customer owes a merchant a sum of money, does not prevent the publication from being libelous if it conveys the additional false implication that the debtor is unworthy of credit." 50 Am Jur 2d, *Libel and Slander,* sec. 179.

The Court expanded on the three-tiered requirement of *Sullivan* in a case decided the same year. In Justice Brennan's majority opinion, the Court said, "a high degree of awareness of...probable falsity" was necessary for a public official to prove libel. *Garrison v. Louisiana,* 379 U.S. 64, 74 (1964). The Court was later to hold that the malice requirement must be proven by clear and convincing evidence. *Bose Corp. v. Consumers Union,* 104 S.Ct. 1949 (1984). The *Garrison* case also used *Sullivan* to discredit criminal prosecutions for libel, formerly justified as a peace-keeping measure when public debates could lead to duels or other violence, stating:

> Truth may not be the subject of either civil or criminal sanctions where discussion of public affairs is concerned... Only those falsehoods with the high degree of awareness of their probable falsity demanded by *New York Times v. Sullivan* may be the subject of either civil or criminal sanctions. For speech concerning public affairs is more than self-expression; it is the essence of self-government.
> *Id.* at 74.

Under these constraints, plaintiffs were forced to prove a statement about them was false and defamatory, but also that the reporters were motivated by "actual malice." Could journalists be questioned about their motivations? In *Herbert v. Lando*, 441 U.S. 153 (1979), the Court declared journalists have no First Amendment privilege to avoid such inquiries, holding that facts about the editorial decision-making process are critical to the plaintiff's action and to meeting the three-part standard set out in *Sullivan*. After *Lando*, journalists had to answer questions ranging along the entire editorial process—questions concerning such journalistic decisions as what leads should be followed, what facts should appear in the finished product, and how much stock should be put in the veracity of sources.

The Court's ruling in *Lando* fueled controversy about the application of *New York Times v. Sullivan*, amid concerns that journalists' First Amendment freedoms would be hampered by the prospect of attorneys probing their innermost thoughts and feelings in search of "actual malice."

Public and Private Figures

By the time the Court ruled in *Lando*, it had already expanded the field of plantiffs governed by the Sullivan decision. *Curtis Publishing Co. v. Butts, supra*, further nationalized defamation law by adding public figures to *Sullivan*'s coverage of public officials and finding that both had to meet the same high standard to prove libel. The *Butts* case involved a defamation suit University of Georgia athletic director Wally Butts brought against the *Saturday Evening Post* for alleging that he fixed a football game.

A 5-4 majority agreed Butts was entitled to the damages he was awarded. But Chief Justice Earl Warren, concurring, sided with the dissenters to do away with any distinctions between public officials and public figures. According to Chief Justice Warren, modern times have blurred the distinction between the two:

> Many who do not hold public office at the moment are nevertheless intimately involved in the resolution of important public questions.... Our citizenry has a legitimate and substantial interest in the conduct of such persons, and freedom of the press to engage in uninhibited debate about their involvement in public issues and events is as crucial as it is in the case of 'public officials.'
> 388 U.S. at 164.

Although they are not curtailed by the threat of electoral controls, Warren wrote that public figures "have ready access to mass media of communications, both to influence policy and to counter criticism of their views and activities.... Public opinion may be the only instrument by which society can attempt to influence their conduct." *Id.*

The Court continued defining the demarcations among defamation plaintiffs in *Rosenbloom v. Metromedia, Inc.,* 403 U.S. 29 (1970). This time, Justice Brennan managed to marshal together a plurality that lumped all public and private individuals under the strict *Sullivan* standard, as long as they were involved in "an event of public or general interest." But in *Gertz v. Robert Welch, Inc.,* 418 U.S. 323 (1974), a 5-4 majority retreated from the *Rosenbloom* plurality to protect the reputational interests of a Chicago attorney defamed by a John Birch Society newsletter. The Court ruled that Gertz was a private individual in the context of the case. Justice Lewis Powell's opinion offered this guide for determining whether a plaintiff is a public or private person:

> For the most part, those who attain [public figure] status have assumed roles of especial prominence in the affairs of society. Some occupy positions of such persuasive power and influence that they are deemed public figures for all purposes. More commonly, those classified as public figures have thrust themselves to the forefront of particular controversies in order to influence the resolution of the issues involved. In either event, they invite attention and comment.
>
> *Id.* at 345.

Gertz allowed the states to determine the appropriate standards for defamation of private individuals, but stipulated punitive damages could not be recovered unless the "actual malice" standard of *Sullivan* was used.

Issues in the Balance

The opinion in *Gertz* shows the Court's continuing attempts to balance the competing issues in defamation cases. In an oft-quoted passage, Justice Powell outlined the importance of the First Amendment and free expression:

> Under the First Amendment, there is no such thing as a false idea. However pernicious an opinion may seem, we depend for its correction not on the conscience of judges and juries but on the competition of other ideas.
> *Id.* at 339-340.

Yet, Justice Powell then noted other interests compete with those of free speech and a free press and that balances must be struck, quoting from an earlier Court ruling in *Rosenblatt v. Baer,* 383 U.S. 75, 92 (1966):

> Absolute protection for the communications media requires a total sacrifice of the competing value served by the law of defamation. The legitimate state

interest underlying the law of libel is the compensation of individuals for the harm inflicted on them by defamatory falsehood. We would not lightly require the state to abandon this purpose, for as Justice Stewart has reminded us, the individual's right to the protection of his own good name "reflects no more than our basic concept of the essential dignity and worth of every human being—a concept at the root of any decent system of ordered liberty. The protection of private personality, like the protection of life itself, is left primarily to the individual States under the Ninth and Tenth Amendments. But this does not mean that the right is entitled to any less recognition by this court as a basic of our constitutional system."
Id. at 341.

In some states, i.e., Michigan, a qualified privilege—requiring proof of knowledge of falsity or reckless disregard for the truth—attaches to subjects of public concern, irrespective of the plaintiff's status as a public figure. See, e.g., *Apostle v. Booth Newspapers, Inc.,* 572 F. Supp. 897 (W.D. Mich. 1983). That approach was specifically rejected as constitutionally based in *Gertz,* 418 U.S. at 346. See also, *Rosenbloom v. Metromedia,* 403 U.S. 29 (1971).

Even with *Gertz* as a guide, courts continued to wrestle with the public or private status of defamation plantiffs. The Supreme Court also made occasional forays into the field.

In *Time Inc. v. Firestone,* 424 U.S. 448 (1976), the Court emphasized that individuals had to "volunteer" to become public figures. Under this requirement, prominent Palm Beach, Florida, socialite Mary Firestone was not a public figure during her divorce proceedings. The Court concluded she called press conferences only to satisfy inquiring reporters and not "to influence the resolution of the issues involved," as required in the public figure standards set up in *Gertz.*

In *Hutchinson v. Proxmire,* 443 U.S. 111 (1979), the Court declared that merely receiving government monies did not qualify one as a public figure and that senatorial newsletters were subject to libel lawsuits. The plaintiff in *Hutchinson,* a scientist exploring the psychological effects of living in space through research on monkeys, brought suit against Senator William Proxmire (D-Wisc.) for awarding the researcher a "Golden Fleece" award. Each month, Proxmire brings attention to persons and enterprises who use taxpayers' money for what the senator has determined are, at best, dubious purposes. Proxmire defended the suit by claiming Hutchinson was a public figure: He received government, or public, funds, and he had media access to respond to the award. The Court disagreed, saying neither government funding nor the opportunity for rebuttals make plaintiffs public figures. According to the opinion written by Chief Justice Warren Burger, Hutchinson "did not have the regular and continuing access to the media that is one of the accoutrements of having become a public figure." *Id.* at 136.

A companion case to *Hutchinson, Wolston v. Reader's Digest Association,* 443 U.S. 157 (1979), denied public figure status to an individual who had been in the news many years earlier. The Court reiterated that judges must determine whether plaintiffs are public or private figures, not juries, citing *Rosenblatt v. Baer,* 383 U.S. 75, 88 (1966).

In *Wolston,* the plaintiff charged the magazine had erroneously identified him as a Soviet intelligence agent, on the basis of his connection to a widely publicized espionage trial 16 years before. Though subpoenaed in connection with that trial, Wolston failed to appear in court because of poor health. He was cited for contempt and received a one-year suspended sentence. The Court ruled Wolston did not thrust himself into a controversy by failing to answer the subpoena, even though his action attracted publicity. Only had he ducked the subpoena to protest the espionage investigation or to influence public opinion would he have qualified as a public figure.

To help them distinguish between *"Sullivan"* and private plaintiffs in defamation suits, courts have devised definitions for "general purpose" and "limited purpose" public figures. A limited purpose public figure is someone who may be eligible for private treatment in one context, but public figure treatment in another. These definitions, from a 1982 case, attempt to incorporate various rulings:

> ...a general purpose public figure... may be defined as a person whose name is immediately recognized by a large percentage of the relevant population, whose activities are followed by that group with interest, and whose opinions or conduct by virtue of these facts, can reasonably be expected to be known and considered by that group in the course of their own decision-making. The relevant population in considering the breadth of name recognition is to be measured by the audience reached by the alleged defamation. The fame or notoriety achieved by a public figure must have preexisted the allegedly defamatory statements which give rise to the litigation.
>
> A limited purpose public figure... is a person who, by voluntary and intentional conduct, has vigorously sought to directly influence resolution of a particular controversy, identifiable as such from the intended audience's perception, resolution of which can reasonably be said to have a perceptible impact on persons other than the immediate participants in the controversy. For a person to be classified as a limited public figure for these purposes, the allegedly defamatory statement must be made within the scope of the particular controversy and must be reasonably related to that controversy.
>
> *Harris v. Tomczak,* 94 F.R.D. 687, 700-701, 703 (C.D. Calif. 1982).

Faced with semantic snakes about such questions as public or private, general or limited, and with judicial balancing acrobatics, one scholar has noted that:

> It must be confessed at the beginning that there is a great deal of the law of defamation which makes no sense. It contains anomalies and absurdities for which no legal writer ever has had a kind word,... The explanation is in part one of historical accident and survival, in part one of the conflict

of opposing ideas of policy in which our traditional notions of freedom of expression have collided violently with sympathy for the victim traduced and indignation of the maligning tongue.
W. Prosser, *The Law of Torts,* sec. 111 at 737 (4th ed. 1971).

Debating Libel

The confusion in the law of libel due to shifting standards applied in different situations cause difficulties for potential plaintiffs and defendants both. Defendants complain about the "chilling effect" on their freedom of expression about matters of public concern when they must worry about the potential of a libel suit, even if they are confident they would be judged innocent of defamation. Libel defendants often face tough sledding in the lower courts and from juries, who are inclined to believe the press already has too much free rein. Litigating to protect their rights can be a major outlay of time and money, and possible media defendants may censor themselves to decrease the chances of that happening. "The threat of being put to the defense of a lawsuit may be as chilling to the exercise of First Amendment freedoms as fear of the outcome of the lawsuit itself." *Washington Post v. Keogh,* 365 F.2d 965, 968 (D.C. Cir. 1966), *cert. denied,* 385 U.S. 1011 (1967).

Those unhappy with the current state of defamation law point to the protracted litigation brought on by *Sullivan* and its progeny as evidence that current forumlas just do not work. Wealthy and powerful plaintiffs can target pesky newspapers with lawsuits, forcing them to close up shop and preventing them from asking too many questions. According to recent reports, the marathon litigation struggle between the Mobil Oil Corporation and *The Washington Post,* two well-endowed corporations, has already cost the newspaper $1.5 million to defend, with no end yet in sight.

Less well-heeled newspapers cannot defend such lawsuits. The *Pt. Reyes Light* was hit with six libel actions engineered by Synanon, a drug rehabilitation organization accused by the small California weekly of having the trappings of a cult. The series won the newspaper both a Pulitzer Prize and lawsuits seeking a total $1 billion in damages. Defending the legal action is beyond the 3,500 circulation weekly's financial resources.

Libel plaintiffs also complain about a chilling effect caused by the current state of libel law. Because so much freedom is accorded to the press, they say, reporters know they can be sloppy in their reporting or can get away with half-truths to make the story more interesting. As a result, individuals who might be the target of such stories are detered from public service and civic involvement. The nation is deprived of valuable leadership because of a fear of defamatory accusations in the press, the critics complain.

And, according to some observers, only an historical accident accounts for the birth of *Sullivan* and its "actual malice" standard. They claim the case went too far and systematized many errors of its own. In 1985, the Supreme Court seemed to agree that there were limits to the reach of *Sullivan*. In *Dun & Bradstreet v. Greenmoss Builders,* 53 U.S.L.W. 4866 (1985), it declared that matters not of "public concern" did not warrant First Amendment protection. Dun & Bradstreet, the nationally known credit-reporting agency, had falsely reported that Greenmoss Builders filed for bankruptcy and distributed that information to five subscribers to its reports. Because of the nature of the publication and the limited audience privy to it, Justice Powell's opinion in the 5-4 ruling declared that it was "speech solely in the interest of the speaker and its specific business audience. This particular interest warrants no special protection when—as in this case—the speech is wholly false and clearly damaging to the victim's business reputation." *Id.* at 4869.

In concurring opinions in the case, other justices voiced misgivings about the current state of defamation law. Chief Justice Burger wrote that *Gertz* and the public figure standard should be overruled; Justice Byron White went so far as to declare the Sullivan case struck "an improvident balance" between the public's interest in being fully informed about public officials and public affairs and the interests of those defamed.

Yet even as *Greenmoss Builders* pushed one category of defamation lawsuits outside of First Amendment protection, Justice Brennan led the dissenters in claiming it did not "obscure the solid allegiance the principles of *New York Times* continue to command in the jurisprudence of this Court." *Id.* at 4873. Brennan referred explicitly to *Bose Corporation v. Consumers Union,* 104 S.Ct. 1949 (1984), a case involving an unfavorable review of stereo speakers in *Consumer Reports* magazine and applying the reasoning of *Sullivan.*

In *Bose,* the Court upheld an appellate court's right to review the findings of a trial court to determine whether "reckless disregard" had been present. Justice John Paul Stevens wrote for the 6-3 majority: "The requirement of independent appellate review reflects a deeply held conviction that judges—and particularly members of this court—must exercise such review in order to preserve the precious liberties established and ordained by the Constitution." *Id.* at 1965.

Critiques and other expressions of opinion have traditionally enjoyed constitutional protection: editorials are classified as "fair comment," and reviews dance around aesthetic questions that cannot be proven true or false. In 1985, the U.S. Court of Appeals reversed a $20,000 libel judgment against a published restaurant review, declaring such writings are "the well recognized home of opinion and comment," subject to personal, and variable, taste. *Mr. Chow of New York v. Ste. Jour Azur S.A.,* 759 F.2d 219 (2d Cir. 1985).

However, when reviews or editorials tread in areas where facts can be determined, they may be subject to libel judgments. This accounts for the trial court's initial ruling in *Bose* and for a 1983 Court of Appeals decision involving *Washington Post* columnists Rowland Evans and Robert Novak, remanding the case back to district court level. In *Ollman v. Evans,* 713 F.2d 838 (D.C. Cir. 1983), the court declared Evans and Novak's 1978 column, normally eligible for treatment as an editorial, was not protected as opinion. The plantiff, a Unversity of Maryland professor, charged that their article destroyed his chances to advance professionally, by implying he practiced Marxist indoctrination in the classroom and by impugning his professional credentials.

In his opinion, Judge Spottswood Robinson attempted to clarify degrees of fact and opinion by saying some expression was a "hybrid" of the two. Such hybrids enjoy an absolute constitutional privilege under *Gertz* only when accompanied by a "full and accurate" narration of the relevant background facts. Robinson felt the editorial at issue unfairly lampooned the professor's reputation, since Evans and Novak did not buttress their case with factual data and even omitted information that ran contrary to their thesis.

A second complaint made about today's defamation law is that plaintiffs unjustly libeled are never fully vindicated in the public eye: this undercuts citizens' respect for public persons and demoralizes society as a whole. Justice White voiced this concern in his concurring opinion in *Dun & Bradstreet v. Greenmoss Builders,* writing that *Sullivan* had polluted the stream of information about public figures, and might allow the media to destroy an individual's reputation and professional life without reasonably investigating the truth of various allegations.

White's concurrence and the overall thrust of the Dun & Bradstreet decision foreshadow future fluctuations in defamation law, as the justices and society continue to balance the right to reputation with the freedom of expression guaranteed by the First Amendment.

OBSCENITY

There's Trouble Right Here in River City

Cast of Characters, in order of their appearance

CYNTHIA BAKER, city council president
THOMAS JORGENSON, legal counsel
COUNCILMAN WILLIAM BROBBIT
COUNCILMAN HENRY RUSK
COUNCILWOMAN BARBARA OLANDER
LORRAINE SMITH, parent
ERNEST WASHINGTON, retired editor of the *River City News*
RICHARD PRICE, president of the Citizens Committee for Public Decency
LINDA WILLIAMS, member of the National Organization for Women
RONALD WILSON, president of American Cable Television, Inc.
ALICE REYNOLDS, civil rights lawyer

A growing pornography industry has emerged in River City, prompting the community to call for action to stem the flow of obscene materials. Today, at its regularly scheduled meeting, the City Council will consider a number of resolutions aimed at dealing with the pornography problem and has invited members of the community to testify at the hearing.

(The resolutions on the next page should be reproduced for the audience who, for purposes of this forum, will act as the residents of River City.)

Ordinance 21-345

RESOLVED, that the city zoning ordinance be amended to prohibit adult bookstores, movie theaters and other adult-oriented commercial activities from being established or transacting business in River City, except in the four-block area bordered by Market, Main, Western and Columbus Streets;

RESOLVED FURTHER, that activities carried out in public view which are demonstrably indecent or obscene are hereby declared nuisances subject to civil control and regulation;

Ordinance 21-346

RESOLVED, that before any municipal license is granted to permit the establishment of a cable television franchise in River City, the city Bureau of Licensing and Permits promulgate regulations strictly controlling the content of cable programming dealing with sexual matters to protect the best interests of the community and to prohibit that which is obscene or indecent;

Ordinance 21-347

WHEREAS: pornography is a discriminatory practice based on sex that has the effect of denying women equal opportunities in society and maintaining a system of exploitation and subordination that materially harms women;

BE IT RESOLVED, that trafficking in pornography, including the production, sale, exhibition, distribution or loan of pornographic material or subject matter, is hereby prohibited in River City, subject to confiscation by the police department as contraband and giving rise to a civil cause of action for damages by any woman on grounds of sex discrimination.

CYNTHIA BAKER, CITY COUNCIL PRESIDENT: Good morning. As president, I hereby call this meeting of the City Council of River City to order. I am heartened that so many members of our community have joined us today to discuss the issues that face our city. As was announced in the newspapers, the City Council met last week in executive session and voted to suspend all other old and new business to concentrate on a problem that threatens the well-being of our community. That problem is pornography. While the members of our council agree that something must be done about the problem, we have not agreed on the solution. Instead, we are asking that you join us in reaching a decision.

Several council members have drafted resolutions that we will put before you this morning. After the resolutions have been presented, we ask that you share your opinions with us. Today, we will truly see an example of democracy in action. To answer any legal questions that come up, I have asked the city's legal counsel to join us. Before we begin our debate, I have asked that he review briefly the law regarding pornography.

THOMAS JORGENSON, LEGAL COUNSEL: Thank you. Under our Constitution, obscene materials can be banned. In the case of *Miller v. California,* the Supreme Court established guidelines for determining what is obscene: First, you must determine whether the average person, applying contemporary community standards, would find the work depicting or describing sexual conduct, when taken as a whole, appeals to the prurient interest; second, whether the work does so in a patently offensive way as specifically defined by the applicable law; and finally, whether, taken as a whole, it lacks serious literary, artistic, political, or scientific value. The Court did give several examples of patently offensive sexual conduct. They included hard-core "representations or descriptions of ultimate sexual acts, normal or perverted, actual or simulated,...masturbation" and certain lewd exhibitions.

Materials that are indecent, but do not qualify as obscene, cannot be banned. They are instead protected as free speech under the First Amendment. It is also important to point out that even if material is obscene, and thus not protected by the First Amendment, a person may not be prosecuted for possessing the material at home. Each citizen's right of privacy protects the private possession of obscene material.

BAKER: Thank you, Tom. We may have questions for you as today's discussion progresses. Now, for the first resolution, I call upon Councilman William Brobbit.

COUNCILMAN WILLIAM BROBBIT: Thank you, Madam President. I rise to introduce a resolution of critical importance to the future well-being of our community. Though you have copies before you, I will read the resolution to you. *(Councilman Brobbit now reads Ordinance 21-345, which appears at the beginning of this forum script.)*

Pornography serves no useful purpose in decent society. It should be outlawed altogether. But some people say we can't simply outlaw this filth. I say those people spend too much time looking at fine print and ignoring what that fine print is doing to a community of upstanding citizens. Still, I don't want to introduce a law that the courts, even wrongly, will undo. So if we can't banish pornography altogether, I have proposed the next best thing. My resolution outlaws porn that is openly inflicted on the impressionable minds of our young, and limits the obscenity industry to a specific location where we can watch them and watch those who patronize disreputable establishments. I organized the first neighborhood watches in River City when we faced a growing crime rate, and I am proud that we were successful in cutting back crime. In the same way, I will organize a citizens' watch to keep track of those who enter the area sectioned off as the "obscenity zone." Let the citizens of River City who patronize or profit from lewd behavior enter that zone at their own risk. We do not want them as our neighbors.

COUNCILMAN HENRY RUSK: I second the proposed resolution, and would like to offer one of my own on a related matter.

BAKER: The chair recognizes Councilman Rusk.

RUSK: Pornography has not only invaded our city but has begun to invade our homes as well. A woman in my council district told me a story that has prompted me to introduce the following resolution: *(Councilman Rusk now reads Ordinance 21-346, which appears at the beginning of this script.)*

Now let me tell you the story that prompted me to introduce this resolution. Some ten-year-olds were having a slumber party in January at a classmate's home. The parents of the child throwing the party supervised the evening's activities. At 8:00 that evening, the young girls received permission to watch television and chose to watch "Family Ties," a popular situation comedy on one of the national networks. While the parents were in the kitchen cleaning the dinner dishes, the girls gathered in front of the television set. As they watched, the television picture was interrupted briefly and the girls were treated to "Passion Play," an obscene movie scheduled on cable TV's "adult" channel.

Now that household doesn't even subscribe to cable TV. Neither the parents of the young hostess nor the parents of the guests would have approved of their children watching such smut. After a few minutes, thank God, the obscene movie faded out and the regular program returned.

It doesn't matter that some people enjoy watching this junk. We are all assaulted by it whether we like it or not. It is imposed on us through advertising in an attempt to increase subscriptions, and involuntarily through so-called "technical difficulties" like the one I described. I suspect some of those so-called difficulties are a form of advertising as well. We have the power to do something about it — and I say it's high time we did.

COUNCILMAN BROBBIT: I second the proposal of Councilman Rusk.

BAKER: Councilwoman Barbara Olander has one more resolution to offer.

COUNCILWOMAN BARBARA OLANDER: What's wrong with pornography, besides the depravity it represents, is that it encourages rape and sexual assault against women. Studies have repeatedly shown that men exposed to pornography are more likely to treat women badly and want to reenact what they have seen done against women. Pornography is a form of sex discrimination against women, because it encourages men to treat them as mere objects for sex and pleasure. I therefore introduce the following ordinance to end the violations of women's civil rights by purveyors of pornography:

(Councilwoman Olander now reads Ordinance 21-347, which appears at the beginning of this script.)

While there are some who will immediately trumpet that the First Amendment conflicts with my proposal, let me tell you that I'm confident it does not. The First Amendment does not protect obscenity, and this is what my resolution is aimed to stop. In addition, the Amendment does not condone discrimination. Justice Felix Frankfurter said that obscenity and group libel were outside the First Amendment's protection. Pornography is both obscene and libelous of women. It is not free speech. We could certainly do something if films and pictures invaded our community depicting blacks or Jews being tortured or mutilated. That the victims in this instance are women should not prevent us from banning this cancer in our society.

Pornography is destructive to all of society, but particularly to women. It cannot be condoned, and it cannot hide behind laws designed to protect ideas. Those laws do not protect criminal activities or sex discrimination. My resolution is the strongest of those offered today, because it is the only one that will banish both pornography and the pornographers.

BAKER: To allow the proposal to receive a full discussion today, I second the proposal. Now, we want to hear from you, the residents of River City. To assist in our deliberations, we will refer to the nuisance and zoning ordinance as Proposal One, the cable television ordinance as Proposal Two, and the sex discrimination ordinance as Proposal Three. I will recognize hands from the audience.

(The following witnesses should be planted in the audience. They do not have to be called in any particular order, with the exception that Alice Reynolds should follow Linda Williams. Any hands from members of the audience who are not among the "plants" should be recognized first to assure the broadest participation. The council president should assist unplanned witnesses when they come up to testify, asking each witness's name and whether he or she is a resident of River City. Council members should feel free to question the witnesses about their statements at any time. Questions add spontaneity and drama to the session.)

LORRAINE SMITH: Members of the City Council, my name is Lorraine Smith. I am a resident of the city, a taxpayer, and a parent with two children in the city's public schools.

I am here today because I think we have a responsibility as citizens to make sure that our city is our own—that is, a pleasant community where we can live productive lives in a clean environment. If we don't take part in our own governance, other outside forces will govern us. That is why I am disturbed by the infestation of pornography in our community. It has a bad influence on children and adults alike. If pornography is socially acceptable, anything goes and civilized society is likely to come apart.

It is time for our city to take a stand on the side of the decent, moral citizens of the community. I support all the propositions before the council if they will end pornography. In fact, I think they should be made stronger. We do not need any obscenity zone in River City. It should be banned altogether. I think we have the legal right to do that. I was told by a lawyer friend, and everything the city's legal counsel said today confirms it, that the Supreme Court has ruled pornography can be banned if it violates community standards. I think we all agree that it violates ours. It is time this community made clear its standards and said "no" to the pornographers. Just as we can ban prostitution, gambling and walking naked in the streets, we can ban pornography as offensive to the public health, safety and morals. We should ban it in the streets and in the television programs that actually enter our homes. Thank you.

BAKER: Thank you for your testimony.

ERNEST WASHINGTON: My name is Ernest Washington, and I am the retired editor of the *River City News*. The proposals before us today concern me. The council, in introducing them, has alluded to the First Amendment, but no one has really talked about it. I'm no lawyer, but I am confident that the courts would strike down each of the proposals offered today as violating freedom of speech and of the press.

The First Amendment was written to protect ideas. It permits us to express our most private thoughts and our most public concerns. It is what permits us to gather in this room today to debate the issues before us. What the First Amendment doesn't do is allow us to pick out which ideas are good and which are bad, allowing people the freedom to discuss only those that have the community's "Good Housekeeping seal of approval."

Pornography may be a problem in our community. But we don't need to kill a fly with a bazooka. That is what the proposals strike me as doing. They threaten the important American values that the First Amendment stands for. The problem with controls on pornography is where to draw the line. What is obscene and what isn't? Who decides? I doubt if the people in this room, concerned citizens all, could reach a consensus.

Are all nude pictures obscene? Then what about the Venus de Milo or other great works of art? Is the depiction of sexual intercourse obscene? If so, many of the recent Academy Award winners, R-rated films, are obscene. I don't think we mean to censor those films. Before we go off outlawing pornography, we have to be aware of exactly what we are doing.

Frankly, I don't see anything wrong with the moral climate of our community. I don't see it being undermined, as some have suggested today. We have a community, everyone here will agree, that we can be proud of. Our schools are considered among the best in the state. Our community supports a diverse cultural atmosphere, including its own theater company, something some of us are especially proud of. I don't want that company to be afraid to put on a certain play because it calls for someone to be less than fully clothed; or our movie houses and libraries, because of these laws, to reduce River City adults to viewing and reading only what is fit for children. If pornography is a problem in the community, we need to find ways of fighting it that do not trample on other people's rights. Only then can we deal with this problem without causing other unintended effects.

Let's remember that adult bookstores and movie houses are already regulated so that their wares are not visible to passersby. No one is forced to patronize them. If you want to get rid of them, don't use them. They only thrive if they're profitable. Similarly, despite the unfortunate incident described by Councilman Rusk, no one is forced to subscribe to the cable adult channel.

The proposals outlined here today would affect all entertainment available to us, as well as hundreds of other things that make our community a rich and fulfilling place to live. I urge you to defeat all three.

COUNCILMAN BROBBIT: Sir, aren't there ideas that are so terrible that we have a responsibility to do something about them? Ideas like murder, genocide, and coups against the government? If these ideas can be controlled, what makes pornography different?

ERNEST WASHINGTON: As I said before, I'm not a lawyer. But, it seems to me merely talking about murder or overthrowing the government, or depicting those things on films or in books, cannot be regulated. Only the *act* of doing those things can be. We already have laws against sexual assault intended to prevent some of the problems that the third proposal addresses.

BAKER: Thank you for your testimony. Let's hear from another witness.

RICHARD PRICE: My name is Richard Price, and I am president of the Citizens Committee for Public Decency, an association of River City residents who are concerned—indeed, alarmed—at the deteriorating moral environment of our city. We are concerned with the quality of our civic life and restoring the foundation of common decency upon which our community rests. We are delighted that the council is finally addressing the problem.

I will speak only to the first two proposals, and not the third, since we do not have a position on it. The Citizens Committee welcomes these resolutions, because they will finally give us badly needed tools to combat the ills that beset us. When passed, these proposals will send pornographers a signal that this community is no longer willing to stand by passively while its most basic values are flouted, its public thoroughfares lined with garish dens of sinful commerce, and its airwaves filled with insults to good taste. Even when covered or hidden, these sleazy and pernicious products are still capable of affronting the senses and sensibilities of passersby. At issue is our very ability, our right as a self-governing community, to make our city a decent place to live.

The CCPD supports the two proposals I address because we recognize that certain products or activities offend the moral sense of the community and thus should be restricted. But we think once you make the decision to regulate pornography, you should also have the wisdom to attack it and eradicate it altogether. If we as a community are offended by the presence of certain kinds of activities and products, why herd them into one part of town instead of railroading them out of town entirely?

Now, I would like to say a word about the argument that we can expect from the liberals. They will jump up and wave their all-purpose banner, the First Amendment, saying we can't make judgments about public decency because all tastes deserve protection. They are wrong. The depraved do not deserve protection of their tastes; the child pornographers do not; the child abusers and the wife beaters do not. These are not matters of taste. They are matters of moral judgment, and it is the obligation of this council to protect the moral fiber of our community. I remind you that the CCPD is an active community organization. If the council will not act to protect us from the smut dealers, then we will elect a council that will. I don't mean to sound threatening, but I want you to know how important we feel this issue is to our city's well-being.

As for cable television, it offers us a unique opportunity to control what comes across the television screen. We all recognize the extraordinary influence of television. What the cable television proposal would do is let us put control over our lives back into our own hands. I ask that the city council pass both pieces of legislation in even stronger language.

BAKER: Thank you for your testimony.

LINDA WILLIAMS: My name is Linda Williams, and I live here in River City. I am only here to represent myself, but I am a member of the National Organization for Women. I support Proposal Three, which I think is the most important of the resolutions.

Whether the law says so or not, pornography is a crime against women. When we allow pornography to exist, we are giving off a message that it is okay to regard women as sex objects, that the desire to rape and accost them is natural, and that women want to be subjugated to men. *All* women are victims of pornography. The first victims are those who are photographed or filmed for pornographic materials. Often they do this out of ignorance of what they're doing or because of financial or social pressures that amount to a violation of their womanhood. Then, the second victims are those who are dehumanized by association just because they are women. When women generally are depicted in such ugly circumstances, all women suffer from the image that is created.

Researchers and clinicians have documented evidence that pornography increases attitudes and behavior of violent, and nonviolent, discrimination by men against women. Pornography is used to break women's self-esteem, to force women into sexual submission, to intimidate them out of job opportunities, to blackmail them into prostitution and to terrorize and humiliate them.

The Surgeon General of the United States, Dr. Everett Koop, has called pornography "a problem with important ramifications for the public health" and "a destructive phenomenon" that "does not contribute anything to society but, rather, takes away from and diminishes what we regard as socially good."

Dr. Koop went on to say that pornography alters normal people, provokes copy-cat rapes, and contributes to domestic violence. It contributes to the rising suicide rate among the young and has a profoundly harmful effect on children. There is absolutely no reason why we should tolerate it.

To argue that pornography deserves the protection given to free speech robs women of the opportunity to exercise fully their right to free speech. Pornography silences women. It is time to stand up for the civil rights of women and stop the conspiracy against them promoted by pornography.

BAKER: Thank you.

RONALD WILSON: I am Ronald Wilson, president of American Cable Television, Inc. As you know, we have submitted a bid to wire River City for full cable access. I'm concerned, of course, about the resolution aimed at regulating cable broadcasts. The words of the resolution, "indecent or obscene," don't really give me as a cable operator much of a guide as to what can or can't be broadcast. Does this include mild swear words in movies, does it include nudity, or what about a couple in bed talking about what they did off-screen? Your lawyer said laws that would ban obscene films have to be specific about what is hard-core behavior. The resolution you have isn't specific. I guess if it were, you could be arrested for obscenity.

The law proposed today is too broad to have any meaning, and I think the courts would think so too. No ordinance in the nation attempting to ban obscene or indecent cable programming has been held up in court.

I make no bones over the fact that we broadcast an X-rated channel. An adult channel is important to a cable operator, because, frankly, it brings in a lot of bucks. Subscribers pay extra to get it. And the rest of you benefit because it keeps costs down for other cable television channels. If community standards are supposed to measure what is acceptable, the adult channel is really okay. It meets community standards. Our experience shows one-third of all cable subscribers opt for the adult channel. Such a large segment of the community deserves a voice in determining what is broadcast. They have rights, too. They vote, in this case, by putting their money where their mouth is, by spending it on an adult channel subscription.

Okay, we've been told the First Amendment doesn't protect obscenity. But it does protect things that are only indecent. Let me give you an example. Adultery may be indecent to some, but it is not obscene. We heard from your own lawyer what the Supreme Court says is obscene. Your law just doesn't comply with what the Court says can be done.

Your proposals don't say what obscenity is, and they don't take into account the possible artistic value in the broadcasts. Instead, they are the kind of flat ban prohibited by the Constitution. I urge that this proposal be defeated before it is struck down in court.

OLANDER: Are you saying that you will sue if we pass the second proposal?

WILSON: Yes, I would sue to have it declared unconstitutional.

OLANDER: Would you also sue if we passed proposal three?

WILSON: Yes. It would apply to us, and I would be obligated to sue.

BAKER: Thank you for your testimony.

ALICE REYNOLDS: I am Alice Reynolds. I have been a civil rights lawyer in River City for ten years. I want to address the proposal that tries to define pornography as sex discrimination, although much of what I say applies to the other proposals as well.

First, this proposal is unconstitutional. It goes considerably beyond the controls the Supreme Court has said are permissible. To decide what is pornographic and, according to Proposal Three, discriminatory as to sex, requires that someone—the courts, a municipal agency—someone act as a censorship panel, deciding what can be read or seen by the public. Personally, I think each individual must decide that for him or herself.

Whenever something defamatory of a woman is depicted, Proposal Three declares, all women are defamed. It then encourages a flood of litigation by self-appointed guardians of women's rights. Worse yet, it helps some try to make a quick buck by suing a movie theater that has no relationship to them at all, claiming defamation against womankind. We don't want to see the courts tied up like this, and we don't want movie theaters to be afraid to book serious movies that might offend some members of the community. What movie theater wants to incur litigation costs and attorney fees, even when it knows it will ultimately be vindicated in court?

Instead, theaters will choose not to show certain popular films, libraries will not keep contemporary fiction, and the community will be deprived of all sorts of cultural stimuli. Even the recent TV movie, "The Burning Bed," would be banned by this resolution because it graphically depicted a woman being abused and assaulted. But that movie is credited with helping people understand and become more concerned about the problem of wife-beating. To ban "The Burning Bed," as the proposal would do, could hardly be described as preventing sex discrimination. I submit that the proposal has nothing to do with discrimination, but it results instead in the sort of damaging censorship prohibited by the First Amendment.

OLANDER: But even your "Burning Bed" example proves my point. A man was convicted of killing his wife by throwing gasoline on her and setting her on fire after seeing that movie on TV. That demonstrates what a pernicious influence a movie that shows women being abused can have, even if done with the best of intentions.

REYNOLDS: I really don't think you can take one example like that and condemn all movies as you have done. I don't know the facts of the case you cited, but it's likely that couple had a long history of abusive treatment, which may have culminated in murder. Who's to say whether the killing would have occurred anyway, perhaps by other means? On the other hand, hundreds of women came forth after the movie to try to take their destinies into their own hands and stop the pattern of abuse that was wrecking their lives.

BAKER: Thank you for your testimony. Are there other witnesses?

(After all witnesses have a chance to testify, or when time is running out, the proposals should be submitted to the audience for a vote.)

BAKER: Today, we have benefited from a full debate on the issues. I would now like to ask the community to give its opinion. Therefore, we'll put each resolution to a vote by a show of hands.
- Proposal One. *(Count hands each time)*
- Proposal Two.
- Proposal Three.

Thank you for your assistance. From the testimony today, it is apparent that determining public policy is a complex process ultimately guided by the fundamental principles of the Constitution; in this case, the First Amendment. We appreciate your participation in this meetings. The council will take your opinions under advisement.

Memorandum on Legal Issues
Obscenity

Obscenity carries with it special qualities that take it outside traditional First Amendment analysis. The emotional and moral reaction to obscenity is so great that it is not regarded as speech. The Supreme Court, in declaring obscenity without constitutional protection, observed that the "lewd and obscene" fall within "certain well-defined and narrowly limited classes of speech, the prevention and punishment of which have never been thought to raise any Constitutional problem." *Chaplinsky v. New Hampshire,* 315 U.S. 568, 571-72 (1942). The Court added, "It has been well observed that [obscene works] are no essential part of any exposition of ideas, and are of such slight social value as a step to truth that any benefit that may be derived from them is clearly outweighed by the social interest in order and morality." *Id.* at 572. See also, *Roth v. United States,* 354 U.S. 476, 485 (1957), ruling "obscenity is not within the area of constitutionally protected speech or press."

Criminal punishments for obscenity did not exist under common law, but they developed in response to the values of the Victorian Age. The first reported prosecution in America occurred in 1857 over the book, *Memoirs of a Woman of Pleasure.*

The courts' principal difficulty has been to define obscenity in a manner that does not infringe upon legitimate speech. The modern law of obscenity was enunciated by the Supreme Court in *Miller v. California,* 413 U.S. 15 (1973). To determine that material is obscene, the Court established:

> The basic guidelines for the trier of fact must be: (a) whether "the average person, applying contemporary community standards" would find that the work, taken as a whole, appeals to the prurient interest, (b) whether the work depicts or describes, in a patently offensive way, sexual conduct specifically defined by the applicable state law; and (c) whether the work, taken as a whole, lacks serious literary, artistic, political, or scientific value.
> *Id.* at 24.

The Court did give several "plain examples" of patently offensive sexual conduct: "representations or descriptions of ultimate sexual acts, normal or perverted, actual or simulated...masturbation, excretory functions, and lewd exhibition of the genitals." *Id.* at 25.

While First Amendment protection is not afforded to obscene materials, the Court has determined "mere private possession of obscene matter cannot constitutionally be held a crime." *Stanley v. Georgia,* 394 U.S. 557 (1969). In *Stanley,* the justices overturned the conviction of a man who kept obscene films at home for his private viewing. Similar treatment of movie theaters showing sexually explicit films was rejected by the Court. *Paris Adult Theatre I v. Slaton,* 413 U.S. 49 (1973).

Though private possession of obscene materials is protected under of the constitutional right of privacy, special considerations are made when the protection of minors is at issue. In *Ginsberg v. New York,* 390 U.S. 629 (1968), the Court upheld the constitutionality of a statute that defined obscenity in terms of its appeal to the prurient interest of minors. A more rigid standard than that employed under *Miller* was found appropriate with respect to child pornography, because of its potential to harm the child and its *de minimis* value. *New York v. Ferber,* 458 U.S. 747 (1982).

However, the Court does not allow these considerations to justify every regulation of pornographic materials. The Court unanimously reversed an obscenity conviction based on a statute that "quarantin[ed] the general reading public against books not too rugged for grown men and women in order to shield juvenile innocence." *Butler v. Michigan,* 352 U.S. 380, 383 (1957). It would not permit the law "to reduce the adult population of Michigan to reading only what is fit for children." *Id.* Similarly, restrictions on outdoor movies cannot be justified on the rationale of protecting passing minors. *Erznoznik v. Jacksonville,* 422 U.S. 205 (1975).

The Supreme Court has steadfastly refused to allow legislation that is designed to prohibit obscenity to be used against ideas. In *Kingsley Pictures Corp. v. Board of Regents,* 360 U.S. 684 (1959), the state denied a license to the movie *Lady Chatterly's Lover* because it favorably portrayed an adulterous relationship, but the Court said:

> What New York has done, therefore, is to prevent the exhibition of a motion picture because that picture advocates an idea—that adultery under certain circumstances may be proper behavior. Yet the First Amendment's basic guarantee is of freedom to advocate ideas. The State, quite simply, has thus struck at the very heart of constitutionally protected liberty.
> *Id.* at 688.

Zoning, Nuisance Laws and Pornography

Zoning laws establish geographical areas where certain types of activities may be conducted. In *Young v. American Mini Theatres, Inc.,* 427 U.S. 50 (1976), the Supreme Court upheld a Detroit zoning ordinance designed to disperse establishments that generally provided adult entertainment, prohibiting adult theaters within 1,000 feet of any two other "regulated uses" or within 500 feet of a residential area. The ordinance specified which depictions of sexual activities and anatomical areas qualified the material as "adult." In finding the ordinance valid, the Court declared:

> the regulation of the places where sexually explicit films may be exhibited is unaffected by whatever social, political, or philosophical message a film may be intended to communicate... Even though the First Amendment protects communication in this area from total supression, we hold that the State may legitimately use the content of these materials as the basis for placing them in a different classification from other motion pictures [which are still subject to local licensing and zoning requirements].
> *Id.* at 70-71.

As the *Young* decision indicates, prohibiting an activity is more than a zoning procedure and is subject to scrutiny and attack for being overbroad. "When a zoning law infringes on a protected liberty, it must be narrowly drawn and must further a sufficiently substantial governmental interest." *Schad v. Borough of Mount Ephraim,* 452 U.S. 61, 68 (1981). The concept of individual privacy permits even legitimate speech to be subject to reasonable time, place and manner restrictions. *Cox v. Louisiana,* 379 U.S. 536, 558 (1965). "To be reasonable, time, place, and manner restrictions not only must serve significant state interests but also must leave open adequate alternative channels of communication." *Schad, supra* at 75-76.

As an alternative to zoning ordinances, municipalities have declared certain activities constitute a public nuisance. Nuisance laws operate to prevent problems that affect the public safety, health, morals, comfort and convenience. While some question whether nuisance laws may be applied to the field of obscenity, a majority of courts appear to accept the proposition "that the exhibition of obscene magazines or films constitutes a public nuisance properly subject to abatement." *People ex rel. Busch v. Projection Room Theatre,* 17 Cal.3d 42, 130 Cal. Rptr. 328, 550 P.2d 600, 607, *cert. denied,* 429 U.S. 1922 (1976); *State ex rel. Ewing v. "Without A Stitch,"* 37 Ohio St.2d 95, 307 N.E.2d 911 (1974), *appeal dismissed,* 421 U.S. 923 (1975). Those decisions hold "that public nuisance laws may properly be employed to regulate the exhibition of obscene material to 'consenting adults.'" *Busch, supra,* 550 P.2d at 606. Still, before an injunction will be issued, the materials must be "adjudged obscene following a fair and full adversary hearing." *Id.* at 610.

In applying nuisance laws, the courts seriously consider the obscenity standard enunciated in *Miller.* In *Erznoznik,* the Supreme Court overturned a law declaring drive-in movie theaters constitute a public nuisance when on-screen nudity is visible from the public street, irrespective of the film's value. The law, the Court said, "sweepingly forbids display of all films containing *any* uncovered buttocks or breasts, irrespective of context or pervasiveness... [even] a baby's buttocks." 422 U.S. at 213.

Restricting Cable Television Fare

The relative scarcity of frequencies on the broadcast spectrum has provided the rationale for affording radio and television lesser First Amendment freedoms than are accorded to the print media. *Red Lion Broadcasting Co. v. FCC,* 395 U.S. 367 (1969). As a result, television is subject to certain kinds of content regulation.

In 1934, the Communications Act, 47 U.S.C. Sec. 151 *et seq.,* created the Federal Communications Commission, giving it jurisdiction over rates, services and broadcast licenses for "interstate...communication by wire and radio." *Id.* at Sec. 157. Commercial cable television was created in 1950 as a fee-generating community superantenna (CATV), enabling viewers to pick up otherwise unavailable signals through a coaxial cable connection or a microwave signal. Because cable television was not transmitted in the electromagnetic spectrum, the FCC was initially denied regulatory authority over it.

But in 1965, the FCC applied signal carriage and nonduplication rules to cable operators. This jurisdiction was upheld by the Supreme Court as "reasonably ancillary to the effective performance of the Commission's various responsibilities for the regulation of television broadcasting." *United States v. Southwestern Cable Co.,* 392 U.S. 157, 178 (1968). The decision merged many of the regulations for cable with those of broadcast television, although the two are not treated entirely alike.

The Court has limited regulatory authority over cable that infringes on editorial discretion. *FCC v. Midwest Video Corp.,* 440 U.S. 689 (1979). Regulations remain valid if they "further an important or substantial governmental interest...and if the incidental restriction on alleged First Amendment freedoms is no greater than is essential to the furtherance of that interest." *United States v. O'Brien,* 391 U.S. 367, 377 (1968). In addition, courts have determined that the "use of public places [including television] for speech-related purposes, although jealously guarded by the First Amendment, is subject to reasonable restraints intended to...prevent 'capture' of unwilling audiences." *Home Box Office, Inc. v. FCC,* 567 F.2d 9 (D.C. Cir.), *cert. denied,* 434 U.S. 829 (1977). In addition, state and local regulations cannot conflict with federal regulations. *Capital Cities Cable, Inc. v. Crisp,* 52 U.S.L.W. 4805 (1984).

While obscenity falls entirely outside First Amendment's protection and can be prohibited on the airwaves, indecent broadcasts are also subject to regulation because of the unique nature of the medium. FCC rules prohibit broadcasting indecent material. These rules were upheld, as applied to radio, in *FCC v. Pacifica Foundation,* 438 U.S. 726 (1978). The dispute in *Pacifica* arose when a parent complained about the daytime broadcast of a monologue called "Filthy Words" by comedian George Carlin. In ruling on the case, the Court declared words that were "vulgar," "offensive," and "shocking" could be prohibited, even if they were not obscene, because the program in which they appeared was broadcast during the day, which made it accessible to children.

To the extent that the FCC does not prohibit indecent cable broadcasts, local regulation appears to be permitted. *TV Pix, Inc. v. Taylor,* 304 F. Supp. 459 (D.Nev. 1968), *aff'd without opinion,* 396 U.S. 556 (1970). In *Home Box Office, Inc. v. Wilkinson,* 531 F.Supp. 986 (D.Utah 1982), a federal district court ruled that since indecent materials are available in other media, a restriction on similar material on cable television channels was disabled. The court also noted parents could control what their children view by purchasing a lock for the television or by changing the channel. Another regulation aimed at controlling indecent cable fare failed to pass constitutional muster in *Community Television, Inc. v. Roy City,* 555 F.Supp. 1164 (D.Utah 1982), because it went beyond the *Miller* obscenity standards. This court ruling also distinguished cable television from radio, as discussed by the Supreme Court in *Pacifica,* because cable television had not become as pervasive as other media.

Similarly, a 1985 Eleventh Circuit decision invalidated a Miami, Florida, ordinance purporting to regulate indecent material on cable television. The court concluded the ordinance was overbroad and reached beyond obscenity standards, did not account for the time of day broadcasts were made or the use of locks to prevent minors from viewing objectionable material, and contained procedures that failed to comport with constitutional requirements of due process. *Cruz v. Ferre,* No. 83-5588 (Mar. 22, 1985)(slip opinion).

Pornography as Group Libel

Recently, certain activists have started a movement that equates pornography with sex discrimination. Ordinances were passed in Minneapolis (where it was vetoed by the mayor as unconstitutional) and Indianapolis defining pornography as the "graphic, sexually explicit subordination of women, whether in pictures or in words" and describing it as "a discriminatory practice based on sex which denies women equal opportunities in society." In the first court test of the Indiana ordinance, it was found to be an unconstitutional infringement of free speech and a unlawful prior restraint. *American Booksellers Association, Inc. v. Hudnut,* 598 F.Supp. 1316 (S.D.Ind. 1984), *aff'd,* ____F.2d____ (7th Cir. Aug. 27, 1985).

The court found no compelling reason to exempt the statute from the *Miller* obscenity standards, holding the special protections given to children in *Ferber, supra,* were not "readily transferable to adult women as a class." *Hudnut,* 598 F.Supp. at 1334. To rule otherwise, would open the door to legislation "prohibiting other unfair expression — the publication and distribution of racist material, for instance, on the grounds that it causes racial discrimination," the court warned. *Id.*

Some observers call such expression "group libel," claiming courts should permit members of a large class of individuals to sue for defamation made on the basis of the grouping. However, courts have largely looked upon this concept with disfavor, and under common law, group libel was not actionable. *The King v. Alme & Nott,* 3 Salk. 224, 91 Eng.Rep. 790 (1699). A singular exception to this rule, of questionable precedential value because of subsequent cases, is *Beauharnais v. Illinois,* 343 U.S. 250 (1952), where the Supreme Court upheld a criminal statute prohibiting the distribution of materials that promoted racial and religious hatred. Speaking for the Court, Justice Felix Frankfurter found no constitutional barrier to group libel laws unless they constitute a "willful and purposeless restriction unrelated to the peace and well-being of the state." *Id.* at 258.

Since *Beauharnais,* however, *New York Times v. Sullivan,* 376 U.S. 254 (1964), was decided, making the First Amendment applicable to libel law. *Sullivan* required libel laws to comport with requirements necessary to give meaning to the freedoms of speech and the press. Although *Sullivan* did not expressly overrule *Beauharnais,* it is difficult to imagine a rationale that allows the latter to remain good law. The Seventh Circuit has "expressed doubt...that *Beauharnais* remains good law at all after the constitutional libel cases." *Collin v. Smith,* 578 F.2d 1197, 1205 (7th Cir.), *cert. denied,* 439 U.S. 916 (1978).

Beauharnais considered the potential for violent confrontation as a factor in validating the Illinois group libel statute. However, restrictions on the content of speech are not permitted simply because that speech might tend to produce violence. Such restrictions apply only if speech "is directed to inciting or producing imminent lawless action and is likely to incite or produce such action." *Brandenburg v. Ohio,* 395 U.S. 444, 447 (1969). The court in *Hudnut* found claims that pornography encourages violence against women were too remote to qualify under the *Brandenburg* standard.

In addition, the potential for offending sensibilities cannot justify restrictions on speech. In *Erznoznik,* the Supreme Court said, "The Constitution does not permit the government to decide which types of otherwise protected speech are sufficiently offensive to require protection for the unwilling listener or viewer." 422 U.S. at 210.

RIGHT TO READ?

Controlling What Goes on School Library Shelves: Censorship or Selectivity?

Cast of Characters, in order of their appearance
CAMILLA JOHNSON, president, Denton Board of Education
ROBERT WIEDRICH, president, Citizens Association for Morality in the Public Schools
DENTON BOARD OF EDUCATION MEMBER NO. 1
DENTON BOARD OF EDUCATION MEMBER NO. 2
EDGAR THOMAS, executive director, Denton Library Association
DENTON BOARD OF EDUCATION MEMBER NO. 3
HELEN HORTHBLOD, Denton resident
MATTHEW HUGHES, Denton resident
WILLARD MASON, Denton resident
ERNEST WEILER, Denton resident
JEREMY RAIN, legal counsel for the city of Denton

In the city of Denton, residents are concerned about the books found on school library shelves. The board of education has called a meeting to examine the issue. One group, Citizens Association for Morality in the Public Schools (CAMPS), has circulated a petition to establish a review board that will choose what books are acceptable, a move they claim will help "restore morality" to the public schools. The board of education has agreed to consider the petition and has invited testimony from the public.

(The CAMPS petition is reproduced on the next page for the audience, who will act as Denton residents present at the board meeting. Forum organizers should photocopy the petition for general distribution.)

A PETITION TO RESTORE MORALITY IN THE PUBLIC SCHOOLS
BY REVIEWING THE BOOKS IN SCHOOL LIBRARIES

We, the undersigned, hereby propose that a citizens board be established to screen all public school library materials before purchase, to determine if the book selections will enhance or detract from the quality of the library's holdings. The board will consider a number of factors, but the decision to acquire a book will rest mainly on its exposition of traditional American social, moral and political values. Inappropriate books would be those that could be termed anti-American, indecent or obscene.

We further propose that this board function retroactively, reassessing books already on the library shelves. All complaints about particular books now on the shelves will be examined in full, so that those complaints may be addressed to the satisfaction of Denton residents and taxpayers.

Those books found to be offensive to certain Denton residents, but also judged to have some redeeming value, will be available to school library users only with the express written permission of their parents or guardians. Students found circulating such books to those who do not have permission to read them will be punished. The punishment will consist of confiscation of the books and a revocation of library privileges for a period of two (2) weeks.

(More than 3,500 signatures of Denton residents follow the three provisions of the petition.)

CAMILLA JOHNSON, PRESIDENT, DENTON BOARD OF EDUCATION: Ladies and gentlemen and board members, as president of the board of education, it is my privilege to welcome you to tonight's meeting. Tonight, we will discuss a subject as important as any that falls within the responsibility of a board of education: what goes on our school library shelves. I am glad to see that so many members of our community have come to the meeting this evening, demonstrating the very real concerns raised by this issue.

The board has received more mail and telephone calls on this matter than any other I can remember. One community group, the Citizens Association for Morality in the Public Schools, has circulated a petition calling for specific controls. That petition, which you have copies of, now has 3,711 signatures.

The concern about the books available to our youngsters in school libraries coincides with increasing concern for the quality of our schools generally. Many of you here this evening know of the recent national studies that have sounded an alarm about the state of American public schools. I believe the petition before us tonight reflects some of that concern and attempts to translate it into concrete action. As with any suggested and potentially far-reaching reform, we must examine all the issues raised closely.

Tonight, we will devote the entire board meeting to this question. Before the board acts, it wants to hear from you, the community. I urge each of you to take advantage of this open forum to express your concerns. Before we open up the discussion, we will hear from two individuals who have asked in advance for time to present their views. First, Bob Wiedrich, president of the Citizens Association for Morality in the Public Schools, will offer his group's viewpoint. Then, Edgar Snow, executive director of the Denton Library Association, will speak. After that, the floor will be open for public comments. Those who wish to offer their views at that time are asked to limit their remarks, so we can give everyone a chance to express an opinion. The board's legal counsel will be available to answer questions on the legal issues raised tonight and what we can or cannot do within the law.

After tonight's discussion, we will conduct a straw vote to see what — if any — consensus emerges from the evening's discussion. So, we ask that you listen to the views expressed carefully. Naturally, this vote will not be binding on the board, although we will use it as a barometer of public opinion. Determining which way the Denton schools go on this issue ultimately determines how we want to bring up our children. With tonight's large gathering, our straw poll can be a reasonably accurate gauge. Thank you for attending.

Now, I'll turn the floor over to our representative from Citizens for Morality in the Public Schools.

ROBERT WIEDRICH, PRESIDENT, CITIZENS ASSOCIATION FOR MORALITY IN THE PUBLIC SCHOOLS: Good evening, friends and neighbors. My name is Bob Wiedrich. I've been a resident of Denton for 23 years, and I am president of the Citizens Association for Morality in the Public Schools, known for short as CAMPS. As you have heard, CAMPS has collected nearly 4,000 signatures on a petition for the appointment of a citizens review committee to place stricter controls on the books in our school libraries. While gathering these signatures, we were amazed by the groundswell of public support. Everyone knows our schools have deteriorated in quality, and the blame can be laid squarely on those who espouse excessively "liberal" philosophies: philosophies and ideas I would wager are actually more "libertine" than they are "liberal."

CAMPS believes the schools should be under the control of the public, and not those who have already failed to do a good job. Teaching in our public schools should reflect good American values and the moral upbringing that we all want for our children. Instead, it is sprinkled with the implied lesson of "anything goes." If parents want their children to have a libertine education, they can send them to a private academy that specializes in that sort of thing. Remember, fellow citizens, we are talking about *public* schools here; your tax dollars pay for these schools, these teachers, these books. Do you want your money to buy books that glorify ideas you don't believe in? In fact, these ideas go against everything you are trying to teach your children.

Several members of CAMPS visited the library at Hart Street Junior High School recently. You would be shocked by some of the books we found there. I would like to share with you some of the examples.

Some of the worst of the books are those by "modern" author Judy Blume. In books like *Are You There God, It's Me, Margaret, Blubber,* and *Forever,* Blume uses sexually explicit scenes to tempt children into reading things they have no business even *thinking* about at their tender ages. She encourages sexual promiscuity by planting ideas in the heads of mere kids. In *Forever,* two high school students have a full-blown sexual relationship that creates feelings and situations they're not ready to deal with at their age. I think most of you would agree that such relationships should be confined to matrimony. Blume also encourages kids to look askance at authority. In *Blubber,* a teacher is referred to as a "bitch." Blume's books are anti-marriage, anti-Christian, and anti-American.

Another book we disapprove of for junior and senior high school readers is *The Color Purple,* by Alice Walker. *The Color Purple* questions both normal sexual behavior and man's relationship to God. It features rape, incest, wife beating, adultery, and explicit examples of lesbianism. *The Color Purple* is a disturbing book that completely deviates from the traditional American philosophy of life.

Ironically, *The Color Purple* is a winner of the American Book Award, even though it subverts the very ideals of our country. Of course, that might not be so ironic when you remember that book publishers are out to make a buck. Books like *Purple* are big moneymakers, using lust and lewd language to lure people in. And the people who hand out book awards are so scared of being called conservative and square that they think being amoral is chic. All of this is just a good example of how so-called "secular humanism" is strangling our society.

Though Americans across the land have voiced concern about the smut that stocks bookstores, right now there doesn't seem to be much we can do about what publishers publish or who gets awards. They've got the money to hire fancy attorneys to defend their empires. Every time someone gets close enough to force them to clean up their acts a bit, they all start screaming about attacks on their civil liberties and their constitutional rights. The only way we can combat them is to acquire airwaves and printing presses for equal time. It's heartening to see that religious broadcasting, even Christian rock groups, are gaining in popularity.

While current interpretations of the law say that we must give the other side its due, we shouldn't have to subsidize them by supplying their books to the libraries of our public schools, where *we* pay taxes to educate our children. Since it's our money that goes into the schools, we should have some say in how it is spent. Citizens for Morality in the Public Schools says it should *not* be spent on smut and filth. That's not censorship—it's just being selective. With just so many educational dollars available, we can't afford to waste them on trash.

The books I mentioned here today are only representative of the filth that is found on our school library shelves. Truly, you would be disgusted and incensed if you saw what every child in this town can easily get his hands on.

CAMPS realizes that we cannot wish away evil or immoral ideas. But we can exercise influence over what is publicly available to impressionable young minds. Adults are able to avoid what they find disgusting, but children don't have the ability to do that. They haven't developed the discretion or sense of right and wrong. When we put filthy or anti-American books in our school libraries, we send a message to our still-malleable children that it is okay to talk dirty or to be unpatriotic or even traitorous. Really, we have to protect children from too much freedom, until they reach the age when they are less susceptible to unwanted influences and beliefs.

We believe the prime responsibility for fostering American values and morality lies in the family. But the school is an extension of family. We want a citizens board made up of parents to act as surrogates for the rest of us, making sure questionable materials do not land on library shelves and become available to anyone who can read. Schools and school libraries should foster a positive sense of our community—of both Denton and America at large. This sense of community must be centered on a common moral pride and dignity.

That is what our petition tries to have this board adopt. Frankly, I don't understand the rancorous debate it has started. The simple fact is that the citizens of the community are paying for books in the schools that are against everything we try to teach in our homes and in our churches. What we seek is only that the school libraries act responsibly, and that parents have a say in the education of their children.

We believe the support you give this petition will be an important first step toward a more sound moral perspective in our public schools. We are working with the *future* of America in those schools. These children are future taxpaying and voting Americans. We must nurture them, giving them pride and a sense of dignity that will make them worthy of the legacy laid by the men and women who fought to make this nation great. CAMPS believes part of this nurturing can be done through reading the right books— books we recognize as classics and books that tell the American story.

I urge you to support our proposals. Thank you.

BOARD OF EDUCATION MEMBER NO. 1: Mr. Wiedrich, do you see this citizens board as an elected or appointed board?

WIEDRICH: We really don't have an opinion on it, as long as parents concerned with traditional values are well-represented on the board.

BOARD OF EDUCATION MEMBER NO. 2: In your testimony, you indicated that you had a preference for books regarded as classics. Isn't it true that some of your members have also attacked books that are regarded as classics, books like *Catcher in the Rye?*

WIEDRICH: I didn't mean to say that calling a book a classic meant it was safe from scrutiny. I think the board should proceed with its work using the best interests of the children as its guide.

JOHNSON: There seem to be no further questions. Thank you, Mr. Wiedrich. Now we will hear from Edgar Thomas, executive director of the Denton Library Association.

EDGAR THOMAS, EXECUTIVE DIRECTOR, DENTON LIBRARY ASSOCIATION: First of all, I would like to point out that I think a debate such as this is healthy; it gives us a chance to reexamine fundamental questions upon which this country is based.

The concerns voiced by CAMPS are very real, and quite legitimate. However, the proposal they have placed before us is patently unconstitutional. Beyond that, certain suppositions running through these proposals are antithetical to what this country stands for. The proposals would enact a tyranny of the majority, suppressing the views of those who were just a bit "off" the proverbial beaten path. This country was founded to prevent a tyranny of one over many, of the royal Crown over the colonists. But our Constitution also protects the minority from the majority, the less-accepted and novel from the sometimes stifling impulses of the old.

Perhaps the most troubling aspect of the proposal is that what it calls a citizens board is actually a censorship board. This board will determine what books are available to be read. Those that don't pass muster are banished. Since no guidelines are established, the board can act arbitrarily in pulling books from the shelves.

That the members of this board are to be citizens, with a selection process yet to be determined, provides no relief from the dangers of censorship. Whenever anyone is entrusted with the responsibility of guarding a community against the "undesirable," it is easier to be overinclusive than underinclusive. That is, it is easier to ban more books than less, so that nothing slips through that could cause an uproar. As a result, censorship can only lead to making less knowledge available to our children in a place—our schools—that is dedicated to the diffusion of knowledge.

Americans put a high premium on "rugged individualism," but censorship puts a premium on conformity. It sees alternative viewpoints and lifestyles through a narrow prism that always finds them wanting. How can we expect to grow and develop, both nationally and personally, if we censure any ideas that are found immoral just because they are unfamiliar?

In actuality, censorship fails to give people credit for being thinking human beings who can make their own decisions. Why would we want to create a nation of automatons, who cannot think on their own? If we Americans truly believe in the ideal of self-government, we've got to realize that only truly informed people, truly alert people, are competent to govern.

Being truly informed does not mean solely an awareness of the good, the "moral," in American life. It's not just knowing the Pledge of Allegiance and all the verses of the Star Spangled Banner. It means being able to look at your country realistically and work towards its improvement. Our system does work, in the main. But it could work better, especially for the more disadvantaged in our society. Some of the books targeted by censors show the lives of the disadvantaged and the disenchanted, those who groups like CAMPS would say exist on the seamier side of life. But that so-called seamy side exists, and we must acknowledge that and devise ways of dealing with it.

I also want to alert you to the fact that the language of these proposals is very vague. What are traditional American values? Can we really agree on the political values that are appropriate in books available to our children? Isn't it too easy, and therefore undesirable, to get caught up in our own political prejudices? Are we going to ban books that portray a president in a bad light? Will we remove a book on political and economic systems that includes objective analyses of communism and socialism?

I think it's obvious that a censorship board would be mired in a morass from which no good can come. I urge you to defeat these resolutions.

BOARD MEMBER NO. 1: Are you saying that every book has a right to be on the shelves of the school libraries?

THOMAS: No, I'm not saying that at all. Of course, books should be carefully selected when they are purchased for a school library.

First of all, librarians are trained to ensure that the books they select are appropriate for certain age groups. A good book has to tread a fine line between challenging children and going over their heads. Second, librarians should be wary of books that operate from a faulty factual premise: transmitting incorrect information results in miseducation, not further knowledge. Third, a librarian should allow for a balance in various perspectives. Kids should be able to sift through the knowledge accumulated over the centuries and come to their own conclusions. We haven't come up with all the answers yet.

In essence, a library should be a house of knowledge that allows a student to be exposed to many points of view. Its books should cover a broad spectrum of subjects and do so in a responsible and professional way.

BOARD OF EDUCATION MEMBER NO. 3: Would you say that only librarians should be involved in the selection process?

THOMAS: No, but they certainly should be a part of it. It would be a waste of a valuable resource, one particularly trained for the task, if schools bypassed librarians and tried to select books without giving great weight to their professional opinions.

BOARD MEMBER NO. 3: Why do you seem to think there is a legitimate role for this citizens board in determining which books should be purchased for the school library, but once a book goes on the shelves they can't touch it?

THOMAS: Selecting books is one thing. But removal of books is another. Certainly, books don't get to stay on the shelves forever once they're selected in the first place. We can't always expand our libraries to accommodate all the latest books, much as we would like to. Still, books should be removed only for the best reasons: a worn edition is being replaced, new scholarship has made the book obsolete, better books or newer editions more adequately cover the subject matter, and so on. They should not be removed because of political or ideological content—that is censorship.

JOHNSON: If there are no further questions, we will open the discussion to the audience at large. Thank you, Mr. Thomas. Those of you in the audience who wish to offer your views on the petition or related topics are reminded that you should identify yourself before you begin.

(To encourage audience participation, the "board president" should first call on members of the audience who do not have predetermined roles. The following roles are designed to supplement any impromptu discussion and insure a full discussion of the issues. The remarks of the first two role-players, both Denton parents, might well be voiced by randomly chosen participants. If so, speakers Horthblod and Hughes may be sacrificed for time considerations. The four pre-arranged speakers need not be called in any particular order, although Willard Mason should precede Ernest Weiler.)

HELEN HORTHBLOD: My name is Helen Horthblod. My family goes to Denton Public Schools. I've listened to both sides of this debate, and I'm still not satisfied. I am worried by those who seem to preach a holier-than-thou censorship, but I'm also a bit annoyed by those who seem to think only librarians can have a say over what gets on the shelves.

On one side, the arguments evoke images of book burnings. Sometimes, the groups that agitate for a clampdown on library material come off as philistines: I get tired of hearing they want to ban classics like *The Diary of Anne Frank* or books by renowned authors like Ernest Hemingway or

John Steinbeck. In order to have impact, literature *is* at times gut-wrenching. Life itself is hardly pretty. Some of these ban-the-books people seem unwilling to truly *feel* and much more willing to whitewash any wonder, novelty, or passion out of the picture.

On the other hand, librarians often seem too busy to truly inspect what goes on the shelves and possibly too out of touch with the kids they're trying to buy books for. They claim they are fairly "neutral." But is there really such a thing as "neutrality" or "objectivity"?

Now I know some authors don't seem to give a wit about their audience, other than as a source of their own income. They have no sense of the wonder of learning they can give to a curious child. A child whose interest in science is kindled by a biography of Jonas Salk will read further from personal curiosity. A child who reads a well-written novel can learn a lot about interpersonal relationships.

Unfortunately, with the books out today, it's no wonder kids don't have any heroes anymore. The main characters are often weak and create more disgust than inspiration. The days of heroic characters seem long gone. You know, some authors have pretty much come out and said they don't care what their books say, as long as kids read them. They titillate teenagers just becoming aware of their sexuality, because the authors know that's what makes books sell. The bottom line in all of this is the mighty dollar.

Although I've picked at both sides, this is not to say that I don't have an opinion. Parents have the responsibility to guide their children. They must take *time* to discuss why they think something is objectionable. For example, they can talk about why a book is obscene. Ask kids what's wrong with the way it depicts the relationship between men and women. What does a good male-female relationship consist of?

Or on politics, why does this book offer interpretations contrary to what we believe actually happened? Children can be taught to be more analytical, to detect discrepancies within and between ideologies.

Get your kids *thinking*. That's what I'm saying. Ultimately, it's the parents, not the teachers or the library, that must do that.

Maybe instead of a censorship board, parents should be invited to meet with the educators and the librarians to talk about these issues. Maybe by getting a better understanding of what each tries to do and the concerns that motivate them, we will all have enough input in the process to make it a happier one for all of us.

JOHNSON: Thank you very much for your remarks. Let's hear from some more people in the audience.

MATTHEW HUGHES: I just want to make a few simple points. I think we as parents... Oh, my name is Matthew Hughes, and I have a son and a daughter in the public schools of Denton. I think parents have a legitimate role in deciding how their children are educated. Too often, we have allowed educational professionals to tell us what's best, leaving us feeling pretty helpless. I want to avoid that problem with the school libraries. Parents should have their say.

At the same time, though, I'm not going to sit in that library and read every book in it. I'm not even going to read every book that anyone thinks about buying for it. I don't think any of us have the time for that. But then I don't completely trust anyone else to do that for me. Not the librarians, not other parents.

This meeting is good because it allows us to talk about our concerns. Maybe we need something like the other parent said to keep a dialogue going. I want my children to read the books that I like, and there are probably books that I don't want them to read. Probably no one else in this room would have the same list of books on either side. Now, I have some control on the books my kids are exposed to because I can forbid the ones I don't like in my house. But kids are kids—if you tell them they can't do something that's the first thing they go out and do. Knowing my kids, if I told them not to read something they'd stay after school or sit in the park to read it, just to find out what all the fuss was about.

I've got another concern: what if the books I *want* my kids to read are taken off the shelves by someone else? Unless I want to go out and start my own library, I can't ensure they'll get to read everything that I might want them to. Sooner or later we have to trust our own children. I just think you should consider that before you start taking books off the shelves.

BOARD MEMBER NO. 2: At what age would you advise us to trust our children's judgment?

HUGHES: You can't pick out an age and simply apply it across the board. Different children develop judgment at different rates. I just think you don't accomplish anything by putting up a "no trespassing" sign over a bunch of books.

BOARD MEMBER NO. 1: But doesn't the board of education have responsibilities in selecting the books? We aren't supposed to turn a blind eye on the situation, are we?

HUGHES: I'm not suggesting you should. But if you are going to exercise responsibility, you need to set up a fair and consistent policy, not simply blot out all publications that might offend someone.

JOHNSON: Thank you, Mr. Hughes. Are there further witnesses?

WILLARD MASON: My name is Willard Mason. I've lived in Denton all of my seventy-odd years. All my kids graduated from Denton High.

I come to meetings like this because I believe in my community, and I believe it's important for us all to be involved with it. I wager that all of you here tonight would agree on that, otherwise you wouldn't be here either.

I'd also wager that you would all agree on more things than you give each other credit for. You all have ideas of right and wrong that are pretty much the same. You all are trying to help your kids grow up to be normal, healthy, happy and law-abiding Americans. You care about your kids, and you'll make time for them: that's why you're here.

Now, it's unfortunate, but some people don't really give a hoot about what happens to their kids. Some kids are an accident in their parents' lives from the start, and any love they get after they're born is an accident too.

What I don't understand is that the people who would use taxpayers' dollars to help these kids out won't get involved in what books they should be reading. The government can step in one place, but another is off limits. It's a contradiction, I think. These people don't want to put any restrictions on obscenity or pornography, but how would they feel if their daughter was raped by someone all fired up on a girlie magazine? I bet they would change their minds real quick.

BOARD MEMBER NO. 1: Mr. Mason, do you have any suggestions on what action the board should take?

MASON: I don't want to tell you what to do, because an old man can lose touch with the world. Each generation has to make its own decisions. But some things are never gonna change. It's like the Bible says: the poor will always be with you. Now I've got nothing against folks who are poor in money, because I've never had much myself. It's the poor in spirit I worry about. Their kids don't get a fighting chance. If you can give people food stamps, you can give kids direction about what they should read.

BOARD MEMBER NO. 1: Now, Mr. Mason, don't you see any difference between giving people the bare minimum for survival — just to keep their body together — and telling them how they should think?

MASON: Harvey, you can't have a sound body without a sound mind. You know that.

JOHNSON: Thank you, Mr. Mason. Are there other witnesses?

ERNEST WEILER: I can appreciate Will Mason's sentiments, because I know they're made with the best intentions. But he is dead wrong.

My name is Ernest Weiler. I know that even the best intentions can become evil in the wrong hands. I saw it happen in the 1930s, when I lived in Germany. I saw the Third Reich take hold of peoples' hearts and minds. In the beginning, there were book burnings. The Nazis burned books like *All Quiet on the Western Front,* because it conflicted with their interpretation of Germany's defeat in World War I. They burned Hemingway's *A Farewell to Arms* and *The Sun Also Rises,* because they showed a Spain different from the Nazi-supported fascism of Franco. As we know, the Nazis didn't stop with book burnings. Millions of innocent people died at their hands. My parents and brother died in the crematorium at Auschwitz.

Some say that the extremism of the Nazis could never take hold here. I say we can never be too wary. Extremist groups are on the rise in this country again.

But it's not only the so-called extremes we must be afraid of. Even the establishment, the majority, can stifle the truth just because it makes them uncomfortable. In the seventeenth century, Galileo's theories on the solar system were banned because they were thought to be heresy. Only recently did the Catholic Church make formal amends with this renowned scientist. We must allow writers, scientists, and anyone who wants to put pen to paper the freedom to explore. Only through this exploration can we push our civilization onward.

I urge you to soundly defeat these resolutions. If you pass them, you will be setting an evil precedent.

(When all speakers have been called on or when time is running out, the president should announce either that no more witnesses remain to be called or that the time allotted for discussion has ended.)

JOHNSON: I want to thank all of you for the interest you have shown in the welfare of Denton. The board will carefully consider all of the testimony we have heard here today. Before we go on to the next item on our agenda, however, I would now like Jeremy Rain to speak to us about the legal ramifications of these resolutions. Mr. Rain represents Denton in most of its legal affairs. Mr. Rain...

JEREMY RAIN: It's my opinion that we'll have no legal problems setting up some sort of a citizens panel, if that's what the board decides is the appropriate action. I think at the very least it's healthy to have an on-going discussion about what our kids are doing in school.

If such a board is set up, however, we have to be very careful about the measures it takes. Court precedents tell us we can regulate what we judge to be obscene. But regulating what CAMPS calls "un-American" works is not going to stand up to scrutiny.

Many of the books that Mr. Wiedrich mentioned have already won court battles, although in one town *The Color Purple* may be used only in a controlled classroom setting.

I will have to discuss the legal ramifications of each resolution in more detail with board members, but I must warn you that we should be wary of overstepping the controls the courts have allowed to us.

Memorandum on Legal Issues
Right to Read?

The First Amendment clearly prohibits the government from acting as a censor. Fundamental to the notion of freedom of speech and of the press is the concept that "there is no such thing as a false idea. However pernicious an opinion may seem, we depend for its correction not on the conscience of judges and juries but on the competition of other ideas." *Gertz v. Robert Welch, Inc.,* 418 U.S. 323, 339-40 (1974). The reasoning behind this concept was eloquently set forth by Justice Louis Brandeis:

> Those who won our independence believed...that freedom to think as you will and to speak as you think are means indispensable to the discovery and spread of political truth; that without free speech and assembly discussion would be futile; that with them, discussion affords ordinarily adequate protection against the dissemination of noxious doctrines; that the greatest menace to freedom is an inert people; that public discussion is a political duty; and that this should be a fundamental principle of the American government. They recognized the risks to which all human institutions are subject. But they knew...that it is hazardous to discourage thought, hope and imagination; that fear breeds repression; that repression breeds hate; that hate menaces stable government; that the path of safety lies in the opportunity to discuss freely supposed grievances and proposed remedies; and that the fitting remedy for evil counsels is good ones.
> *Whitney v. California,* 274 U.S. 357, 375-76 (1927)(Brandeis, J., concurring).

Past efforts to restrict books have largely been over those judged obscene. Because obscenity is not protected by the First Amendment, *Roth v. United States,* 354 U.S. 476 (1957), obscene books may be regulated and even enjoined from distribution. *Kingsley Books v. Brown,* 354 U.S. 436 (1957). The Supreme Court has said, "It has been well observed that [obscene works] are no essential part of any exposition of ideas, and are of such slight social value as a step to truth that any benefit that may be derived from them is clearly outweighed by the social interest in order and morality." *Chaplinsky v. New Hampshire,* 315 U.S. 568, 572 (1942).

However, the Supreme Court has ruled that obscenity is to be narrowly defined, and materials must be judged obscene before they can be censored. *Miller v. California,* 413 U.S. 15 (1973).

These requirements cannot be evaded by using advisory lists of books that are considered indecent. For example, Rhode Island once had a commission to educate the public about books and other publications with "obscene, indecent or impure language," or "tending to the corruption of the youth." Supposedly, the commission intended only to seek booksellers' cooperation in restricting distribution of undesirable publications, but it circulated lists of these publications to police departments. The Supreme Court saw this scheme as a subterfuge that attempted to evade the requirements for banning obscenity, declaring it unconstitutional as "state censorship effectuated by extralegal sanctions." *Bantam Books v. Sullivan,* 372 U.S. 58, 72 (1963).

The First Amendment in the School Setting

Books that are not obscene enjoy constitutional protection: "the State may not, consistently with the spirit of the First Amendment, contract the spectrum of available knowledge." *Griswold v. Connecticut,* 381 U.S. 479, 482 (1965). Still, additional considerations are in order when applying the standards to schools and students. In invalidating an Arkansas law that prohibited the teaching of Darwin's theory of evolution, Justice Abe Fortas observed:

> Judicial interposition in the operation of the public school system of the Nation raises problems requiring care and restraint. Our courts, however, have not failed to apply the First Amendment's mandate in our educational system where essential to safeguard the fundamental values of freedom of speech and inquiry and of belief. By and large, public education in our Nation is committed to the control of state and local authorities. Courts do not and cannot intervene in the resolution of conflicts which arise in the daily operation of school systems and which do not directly and sharply implicate basic constitutional values. On the other hand, "[t]he vigilant protection of constitutional freedoms is nowhere more vital than in the community of American schools." *Shelton v. Tucker,* 364 U.S. 479, 487 (1960). As this Court said in *Keyishian v. Board of Regents,* the First Amendment "does not tolerate laws that cast a pall of orthodoxy over the classroom." 385 U.S. 589, 603 (1967).
>
> *Epperson v. Arkansas,* 393 U.S. 97, 104-105 (1968).

A major goal of schools is to socialize children, so that they will be able to function within society. However, while it is "easy to appreciate" the "desire of the legislature to foster a homogeneous people with American ideals prepared readily to understand current discussions of civic matters," *Meyer v. Nebraska,* 262 U.S. 390, 402 (1923), some things lie beyond government's regulatory jurisdiction. Thus, in *Meyer,* the Court invalidated a Nebraska statute requiring school instruction only in English.

In *Tinker v. Des Moines Independent Community School District,* 393 U.S. 503 (1969), the Supreme Court struck down a school disciplinary rule enforced against students wearing black armbands to protest government policies in Vietnam. In finding the bands constituted symbolic speech, the Court declared, "It can hardly be argued that either students or teachers shed their constitutional rights to freedom of speech or expression at the schoolhouse gate." *Id.* at 506.

The Supreme Court faced the constitutional question raised by removing school library books in *Island Tree Union Free School District No. 26 v. Pico,* 457 U.S. 853 (1982). In September 1975, three board of education members sought action on a list of books considered objectionable by the politically conservative sponsors of a conference the three had recently attended. The board, the following February, gave an "unofficial direction" that ten books be removed from the school libraries, so that board members could read them. When the board's action attracted attention, members responded with a press release describing the books as "anti-American, anti-Christian, anti-Semitic, and just plain filthy."

The books on the list included *Slaughter House Five* by Kurt Vonnegut Jr.; *The Naked Ape,* by Desmond Morris; *Down These Mean Streets,* by Piri Thomas; *Best Short Stories of Negro Writers,* edited by Langston Hughes; *Go Ask Alice,* anonymous; and *Soul on Ice,* by Eldridge Cleaver.

Eventually, the board appointed a review committee that recommended five of the books be returned to the library shelves, two be placed on restricted shelves, and two be removed entirely. No recommendations were made for the remaining book. The full board voted to remove all but one, giving no reason for its action.

At this point, several students filed a lawsuit that claimed their First Amendment rights had been violated by the board's action. The students' position was summarily rejected by the federal district court, but the Second Circuit ordered the case remanded for a full trial. By a 5-4 vote, with seven separate opinions, the Supreme Court affirmed.

While the fractured nature of the Court's decision left more questions open than were answered, a clear majority of the justices agreed that school boards do not have unrestricted authority to select library books and that constitutional rights are implicated when books are removed arbitrarily. Justice William Brennan, joined only by Justices Thurgood Marshall and John Paul Stevens, wrote a plurality opinion setting up a test for decisions on book removals:

> If petitioners *intended* by their removal decision to deny respondents access to ideas with which petitioners disagreed, and if this intent was the decisive factor in petitioners' decision, then petitioners have exercised their discretion in violation of the Constitution. To permit such intentions to control official actions would be to encourage the precise sort of officially prescribed orthodoxy unequivocally condemned [by this Court before].
>
> *Id.* at 871.

Only Chief Justice Warren Burger, in dissent, claimed school authorities had unbridled discretion in selecting or removing books. An overwhelming majority of the Court condemned politically motivated book removals. On the other hand, the Court strongly suggested decisions based on educational suitability would be upheld, particularly where a regular system of review with standardized guidelines had been adopted.

Justice Brennan's opinion distinguished between acquiring and removing books, in effect giving already-purchased books a "tenure" of the sort that teachers often covet. The Court specifically did not address the question whether any rights were involved when a school board refused to purchase a particular book. Some of the other justices saw the plurality's distinction between acquisition and removal as a semantic balancing act, but they did concede that the act of removing a book from a library with any empty shelves was inherently suspect. In contrast, to limit the purchase of books with an eye to such practical considerations as limited funds was considered beyond reproach. Justice Brennan also attempted to set up a related First Amendment right to receive information as being inherent in the right to express oneself. However, this notion did not command a majority of the Court.

The dissenters reasoned that the school board had not placed any real restraints on what students could read, since any books banned in the school library were available at public libraries. They also argued that "random" vulgarity should be enough to remove a book from school library shelves and that authorities need not show a book was "pervasively" vulgar, in contrast to the norms for obscenity outside of the realm of the schools.

FREEDOM OF ASSEMBLY
AND GROUP LIBEL

Nazis March on Libertyville

Cast of Characters, in order of their appearance:

FRANCES WHITCOMB: Libertyville council president
BENJAMIN MAYER: Libertyville council member
LIBERTYVILLE COUNCIL MEMBER No. 1
RUDOLF GALE: Party of American National Socialists
LIBERTYVILLE COUNCIL MEMBER No. 2
LIBERTYVILLE COUNCIL MEMBER No. 3
GERALD KOEHLER: Libertyville Chief of Police
BRIAN HUPERT: Anti-Defamation League member
DAVID GREEN: Libertyville Civil Liberties Union member
MARY WILSON: Libertyville resident
WALTER WILLIAMSON: Editor of the *Libertyville News*
BARRY NEWMAN: Legal Counsel for Libertyville

Libertyville is a suburb of a major metropolis, Megacity. While for some residents it is but a bedroom community, Libertyville has retained a distinct financial and intellectual life, the latter due in part to a number of colleges within its city limits.

Libertyville boasts a diverse population with a contingent of intellectuals and pockets of ethnic groups that mirror the larger ethnic communities of Megacity. However, in contrast to the ghettos of Megacity, the standard of living in Libertyville is fairly uniform — and fairly comfortable.

One of the larger ethnic pockets in Libertyville is comprised of Jews, whose roots there extend back to the late nineteenth century. Because its Jewish community had always been a large and stable force in Libertyville, it became a haven for survivors of the Nazi holocaust of World War II.

Partly because of Libertyville's noticeable Jewish population, the Party of American National Socialists (PANS), a neo-Nazi group, announced it would march there, but promised the march would be peaceful and follow all city regulations.

Despite such promises, many Libertyville residents want to prevent the march. Councilman Benjamin Mayer, whose entire family perished in the

Nazi holocaust, has written a number of resolutions to stop the march. The town council has called a special meeting to discuss the PANS demonstration and Councilman Mayer's resolutions.

(This community forum, a mock council meeting, will consider Councilman Mayer's resolutions and what can and should be done about the Nazi march in Libertyville. The resolutions are reproduced below, so that forum organizers may photocopy them for distribution to participants and the audience.

The council president will moderate the forum, following the directions as they appear in the text. In general, forum participants are encouraged to improvise questions for both "planted" and impromptu witnesses to stimulate debate and add drama to the forum.)

ORDINANCES INTRODUCED AT A SPECIAL MEETING
OF THE LIBERTYVILLE TOWN COUNCIL

Ordinance 7001
WHEREAS: the announced march by the Party of the American National Socialists has inflamed public opinion and threatens the danger of violence in Libertyville,
BE IT RESOLVED that the Party of the American National Socialists not be issued a permit to march in Libertyville, on April 20 or on any other date.

Ordinance 7002
RESOLVED that all parties planning parades, marches, protests, or demonstrations must obtain a city permit, issued a minimum of 30 days in advance of any such event. Permits shall be issued only after the organizers obtain public liability insurance in the amount of $1,000,000 and property damage insurance in the amount of $500,000, protecting the city from unforeseen expenses which might occur in connection with the event.

Ordinance 7003
RESOLVED that it be unlawful for any individual or group to speak or disseminate materials which engage in group libel, leveling malicious and false charges at individuals of one sex, race, religion, or ethnic group.

FRANCES WHITCOMB, LIBERTYVILLE TOWN COUNCIL PRESIDENT: Good evening, ladies and gentlemen and members of the Libertyville Town Council. As president of the council, I now call this special meeting to order. We have gathered tonight to discuss an item of controversy, a proposed march by members of the Party of American National Socialists, more familiarly known as the Nazi Party.

At the outset, I would like to register my own disgust for the philosophies of this organization, a replica of the German Nazi Party which brought the world the horror of the Holocaust during World War II. Their beliefs and creeds are repugnant to any civilized human being.

While many find the Nazis' ideals abhorrent, it is imperative that we maintain clear heads and a sense of order through the course of this meeting. That includes allowing those who have requested an opportunity to enjoy the freedom to speak their mind. Everyone here has a right to his or her personal opinion. We will hear everyone out.

After Councilman Mayer introduces the proposed resolutions, the floor will be open for testimony and comments from the citizens of Libertyville. We ask those who speak to be concise and to-the-point so that all who wish to give their opinion can do so. We also ask that speakers identify themselves and any institutional affiliation they might have.

The Libertyville council will try to consider the testimony of those here tonight in determining how this issue will be resolved. That's why we've called this special meeting: to listen to all of you and to clear the air. We want to *talk* this situation into a rational resolution.

Whatever the intentions of you here assembled, I must remind all of you that our options might be limited by law. To advise us as to those concerns, I have invited Barry Newman, legal counsel for Libertyville, to speak to us at the conclusion of this meeting.

All right. Councilman Mayer, you may introduce your resolutions at this time.

COUNCILMAN BENJAMIN MAYER: Thank you, Madam President. I introduce the resolutions that have been distributed among you not as a Jew, but as a representative of everything decent in man. We enjoy a good community, a place where we can live and raise our children among good and caring neighbors. Now a cancer threatens the community we all cherish.

This cancer comes in the form of the Party of American National Socialists, who have vowed to march in Libertyville on April 20 to commemorate Adolf Hitler's birthday. Party members have already distributed flyers throughout the metropolitan area that urge extremists to descend on our city.

In order to prevent this disruptive influence in Libertyville, I have written several resolutions to be introduced at this time. They were composed to prevent this cancer from sapping the spiritual life of Libertyville. I will read them aloud now.

(Mayer now reads the resolutions that appear at the beginning of this forum script.)

To prevent this tragedy—this cancer—from infecting our community, I urge your full support for these resolutions. Otherwise, we will all be partners to the Nazis' travesty of truth and history.

The first resolution outlaws the planned march, the other resolutions presented would allow us to prevent similar ugly occurences in the future. They would give us the means to control who shall speak in our streets.

Council members and citizens of Libertyville, we cannot allow the vile doctrines of these Nazis to pollute our streets and the minds of those among us who can be swayed by base persuasion. Listen to one of the flyers they are posting around Megacity: "We will march in areas of heavy Jewish concentration, where by now good American citizens have realized that we have to rid our country of these bloodsuckers." Their speech is obscene and it is not protected by the U.S. Constitution. The justices of the Supreme Court have allowed municipalities to ban obscenity within their borders; Libertyville should take this opportunity to do so.

I ask you, citizens of Libertyville, have we not learned from the lessons of Auschwitz, of Bergen-Belsen, of Dachau, of Treblinka? Have we not learned from the six million?

Forty-two of those six million were members of my family. They died, starved and stuffed into railway cars. They died, gassed at the crematoria. The horror that became the Holocaust was allowed to happen because the world sat still. It continued to happen because the world could not believe it was happening. They refused to believe that men were capable of such inhumanity to other men. If we allow the Party of the American National Socialists to spread its doctrines here in Libertyville, we would allow the Holocaust to happen again. I, for one, cannot sit still at home on April 20 with my wrenching memories, waiting for the deportations and the persecutions to begin anew.

I have talked to many Jews who do not plan on hiding from the Nazis any longer. Their anger at the unspeakable is being unleashed after decades, and they say they do not know what they will do. If the Nazis march, these people will be there. I cannot say what they will do.

But it is not only we Jews who say "never again." The whole world remains stunned by the scope of the madman Hitler's dream and recoils from that nightmare. We *all* must continue to join to prevent the Nazis from sullying our streets and our minds! We cannot sit back and allow them to fragment our community and drive us apart. It is only through such division that the Nazis were able to lay the foundations for what they had hoped would be the Third Reich of Germany. They picked on the Jews as a scapegoat. Instead of giving the German people something to rally around, they gave Germany something to rally against. We must show today's Nazis that Americans do not need such sour dreams.

Support these resolutions, citizens of Libertyville. You must not allow our community life to be perverted by these purveyors of hate.

LIBERTYVILLE COUNCIL MEMBER NO. 1: I second the resolutions proposed by Councilman Mayer.

PRESIDENT WHITCOMB: Thank you. Because this issue is of such wide community concern, we want to open the discussion to you, the citizens of Libertyville. You must live with our decision in this matter, so you should be a part of it now.

Several individuals have asked in advance for permission to make a statement. We will allow them to start the discussion. I remind witnesses that they should first introduce themselves and state their affiliation with any institution or group. Also, council members may question witnesses about the statements they make. Our first witness will be Rudolf Gale.

(Rudolf Gale and the other witnesses included in this script will be planted among the forum participants. However, after Mr. Gale and Chief Koehler speak, the council president should first recognize the hands of unplanned witnesses in the audience to ensure the broadest possible participation in the forum. Other planned witnesses should be heard before the close of the forum.

As noted before, the council president will assume responsibility for moderating the meeting, selecting witnesses, and thanking them for their testimony. The president should require both planted and impromptu speakers to identify themselves and their affiliation before they give testimony. Council members may freely question all witnesses.)

RUDOLF GALE: My name is Rudolf Gale. I am director of education for the Party of American National Socialists. It is my organization that wishes to hold a demonstration in Libertyville on April 20.

In the resolutions proposed here today, you see a perfect example of what our party is trying so desperately to warn you against. The Jews are choking our government from within, choking it in Libertyville and choking it at the national level. In Libertyville, you are forced to kowtow to old men who make peevish demands. We've all seen pictures of President Reagan trying to mollify New York rabbis. Luckily, Reagan refused to acquiesce to their ridiculous demands at Bitburg, when they tried to humiliate him. The actions of the Jewish cabal at Bitburg were designed to separate us from our German allies and make it easier for godless communism, which they not-so-secretly support, to take us over. Everywhere, the Jews force us to hold to illogical policies that will inevitably bring about their worldwide triumph.

The Jews have orchestrated a worldwide communist conspiracy that aggrandizes their own positions. Who do you think was responsible for the oil embargo and for our problems in the Mideast? The Jews! Who do you think incited their black friends to the riots that threatened the stability of this country in the 1960s? The Jews! The whole story of the so-called "Holocaust' is a elaborate distortion, concocted to beg sympathy and blind you to the insidious dealings of these people.

COUNCILMAN MAYER: *(jumping to his feet)* I object! How can this man say the Holocaust was a lie when we have the proof of thousands of bodies? When the Allies marched into the camps, they found not only the thousands of bodies of the dead, but also those of the living dead — liberated long enough to whisper of the horrors and then to die.

GALE: You see, he will not even let me speak my piece.

PRESIDENT WHITCOMB: Councilman Mayer, we recognize your objection. Please allow Mr. Gale to continue. Mr. Gale, please confine your remarks to the resolutions at issue.

GALE: The Jews try to discredit anything they didn't do or anything they can't control. They try to discredit Adolf Hitler for creating an economic and political miracle, for bringing Germany back to its feet. They did not care about the future of the Fatherland, but only about how fat their own purses were.

PRESIDENT WHITCOMB: If you don't address the resolutions, I will have to ask you to step down.

GALE: Very well. The Jews, through these resolutions, would strangle our speech and prevent us from telling you and the world the truth. We will *not* be silenced. The Jew, the conduit for the communism that threatens the world, forgets we true Americans do still have our liberties. In the United States, we have the right to freedom of speech. The First Amendment protects us, and it protects the truth. How can the Jew deny us the First Amendment, when he and his big media friends so often hide behind it?

Our march in Libertyville will be within the bounds of what is permitted under the First Amendment. We will be orderly and nondisruptive. Your resolutions will not stop us. The march will go on.

PRESIDENT WHITCOMB: Mr. Gale, are you saying that the march will go on even if the town council legally prohibits it?

GALE: Yes, it will.

COUNCIL MEMBER NO. 2: Mr. Gale, are you a citizen of Libertyville?

GALE: No, I'm not. The Party of the American National Socialists is headquartered in another suburb of Megacity. But the ideals of the party are applicable everywhere.

COUNCIL MEMBER NO. 3: Mr. Gale, does your party believe in the Constitution of the United States?

GALE: Of course. I've just finished saying that the First Amendment protects my freedom to tell the world the truth about the Jews and about history.

COUNCIL MEMBER NO. 2: All right. How about the First Amendment's provision to protect freedom of religion? Does that square with your attitude toward those of the Jewish faith? When you talk about "godless communism," does that mean your party believes in any sort of religion?

GALE: The "godlessness" of communism makes everything the same. It ignores the genetic and cultural superiority of those who are meant to be leaders. The Jews are not only a religion, they are a race—a genetically inferior race, at that. That's why Hitler wisely tried to weed out even those Jews who had forsaken their heritage and pretended to be Aryan. They would have polluted the genetic pool. And that's what we're seeing in the United States and in the world today: a bastardization of the human race.

PRESIDENT WHITCOMB: That is quite enough, Mr. Gale. Our next witness will be Gerald Koehler, the Chief of the Libertyville Police. Mr. Koehler...

GERALD KOEHLER, LIBERTYVILLE CHIEF OF POLICE: I'm Gerry Koehler: twenty years on the police force in Libertyville and chief for the last seven. I've asked to talk to you tonight because I'm pretty worried about whether my men can control the kind of demonstration this Nazi party is talking about. We're really not worried so much about the politics of all this: just the possibility of violence. There are rumors of a counterdemonstration by outsiders that might get out of hand and do bodily harm to Gale's gang.

I'm not telling you what to do here. All I'm saying is that I want to keep the peace. If the best way to do that is to prevent Gale and his group from demonstrating in Libertyville, then maybe that's the way we should go. In the long run, that might actually be for the Nazis' own good. There are a lot of old wounds in Libertyville with angry scars. The Nazis are really the ones who could get hurt.

If you don't decide to ban the Nazis from Libertyville, I'm going to need the go-ahead for mobilizing more of my force that day. I think we have to prepare for the worst so my men aren't surprised and unable to control the crowd. Of course, we'll do everything in our power to prevent fists or worse from flying, but emotions can get out of control here. There's no telling what could blow up in our faces.

Another thing is both sides are dragging in fanatics from across the country. We've picked up flyers around town that talk about "smashing the fascists." I think militant Jewish groups are planning more than just peaceful counterdemonstrations.

This whole situation has, as I said, gotten completely out of hand. If you want to know what I think, I think the best thing the town council can do is take matters in its hands right now. You can prevent this town from becoming a battleground for someone else's political struggle. The worst thing about this whole problem is that it's been brought in by outsiders and makes our own folks the victims.

Well, I've had my say. All I ask of you council members is that you do what you do what you can to help me keep the peace in Libertyville.

PRESIDENT WHITCOMB: Thank you, chief. Now I will open the floor to any who wish to testify.

(Both previously planted witnesses and brave souls from the audience should be called upon. The following witnesses should be prepared to assure all points of view.)

BRIAN HUPERT, ANTI-DEFAMATION LEAGUE: My name is Brian Hupert, and I'm with the Anti-Defamation League. I would like to echo the sentiments of both Councilman Mayer and Police Chief Koehler in telling all of you that this march must not occur. If you are so foolhardy as to allow it to go through, I cannot predict what will occur. I consider myself one of the most calm of my compatriots at this point, and I can barely sit in the same room with someone as repugnant as Rudolf Gale. To allow him and his ilk to use the streets of Libertyville to spread their filth only sanctions their ugly preachings.

As I said, I consider myself allied with the more calm elements who are considering possible counterattacks on this issue. We have commitments on the part of 50,000 people to show up for a counterdemonstration on April 20. We will honor the dead of the death camps, chanting the names of those houses of horror. Our voices and theirs will overpower the ugly posturing of the Nazis and expose their inhumanity and insanity to the world.

We Jews here in Libertyville, who have perhaps the most obvious personal stake in this demonstration, will be joined by many others who deplore the dehumanization of the Nazi nightmare. Members of Christian congregations throughout the city will demonstrate their solidarity with us by wearing a yellow Star of David, reminding us of the deathly discrimination practiced in the Third Reich.

While we believe the might and right of our combined voices will drown out the Nazis, we still implore you to take action to avoid forcing a confrontation. Those of us who do plan measured resistance to the Nazi message do not know if those who are stridently vengeful can be controlled. They will let their emotions rule. They believe they must strike back at the Nazis. They *live* the credo "never again." They will not let Jews be led wholesale to their own slaughter.

I urge you to avoid the ugliness of this confrontation. Do not let the Nazis sully the name of Libertyville or create havoc and violence in our streets. Prevent them and others like them from marching.

DAVID GREEN, LIBERTYVILLE CIVIL LIBERTIES UNION: I'm David Green, with the Libertyville Civil Liberties Union. First, I must emphasize that my colleagues and I find the ideas expounded by Rudolf Gale and his followers to be morally reprehensible, deserving our most concentrated contempt. However, we are obligated to uphold the freedom of speech of Gale and his fellow Nazis. If we do not do so and allow anger to deny them this freedom, we lay the groundwork for the denial of our own freedom sometime in the future.

I ask you, if we once start to allow incursions into anyone's civil liberties, how can we insure that our own are protected? Who is to determine what can be censored and what is "protected" speech? If Libertyville were a Southern town in the early 1960s, considering resolutions to outlaw a proposed civil rights march, would we feel the same way?

Actually, Gale and his fellow Nazis provide Libertyville with a unique opportunity to show once again that it is a center for intellectual freedom. By allowing the Nazis their say, Libertyville can demonstrate that it stands for the most basic of liberties protected by the U.S. Constitution. Through its soul of sensitivity and rationality, Libertyville can show the folly of these doctrines of hate. Only through frank, open discussion of the polemics involved here can we demonstrate what *is* the truth. This is also the best way to insure we will "never again" see the horror of the Holocaust. We can use the ugliness of these American Nazis today to educate our young people about the folly of history.

Although I can understand the anger and frustration of those for whom Brian Hupert speaks, I must urge you to channel those emotions into creative and effective protest instead of violence. Only through the free flow of ideas will the truth win out in the end.

We achieve nothing by denying the Nazis the freedoms guaranteed to us all by the U.S. Constitution; instead, doing this would sink us to their level of degradation. If we allow ourselves that corrupting luxury, we become the oppressors.

Only through reason and rationality can we resist these horrors and educate the world about them. We depend on the rule of law to protect us from new incarnations of a Hitlerian world. We must rely on that rule of law—upon the U.S. Constitution, upon the exchange of ideas—to protect us from such a horror. But as we are protected, we must realize those doctrines and ideologies that we abhor are also protected.

The First Amendment of the U.S. Constitution protects Rudolf Gale and his followers as surely as it protects you or me. But this does not mean we must resign ourselves to letting Mr. Gale project his views uncontested. Use your freedom of speech to point out the Nazis' lies and to teach people about the Holocaust and the importance of a tolerant and thoughtful society. Use your freedom to insure that the beliefs of Adolf Hitler and Rudolf Gale will "never again" gain political ascendency. Thank you.

PRESIDENT WHITCOMB: Thank you. Are there other witnesses?

MARY WILSON: I am Mary Wilson. I've lived in Libertyville all my life. I have three children, two boys—one eleven and one four—and a daughter who is eight years old. I don't want to give a speech. Enough people have done that already. What the police chief said frightens me. If you let this march happen, I will be forced to keep my children at home that day. I don't want them to be innocent victims of violence when a riot breaks out. All I have heard today is about freedom for the marchers. What about our freedom? I mean, my and my children's freedom to walk the streets and to play in the park and to go to school without being afraid that we will get caught up in a fight that doesn't even belong in Libertyville. We, as law-abiding citizens who chose to live in a peaceful community, must have some rights, too. Well, that's all I wanted to say. I think you have to consider our freedom too.

WALTER WILLIAMSON, EDITOR, LIBERTYVILLE NEWS: I was reluctant to come up here today. Oh, I'm Walter Williamson, editor of the *Libertyville News*. I was reluctant to come up here because I get my say in our editorials, and I sometimes think those of us in the news business too often consider ourselves special guardians of the First Amendment. Nevertheless, I feel I must speak.

Newspapers like to believe, and time has seemingly borne out this belief, that we perform an essential function in maintaining a free and open society. Only in that kind of society can citizens have the information they need to make intelligent choices and to engage in the kind of robust debate that allows us to test ideas before we embrace them. As our world becomes ever more complicated, and as nations and peoples become ever more closely linked, a free flow of information is critical. We need to understand each other better, which can happen only if everyone's speech is free, even those with hateful messages. As long as speech is free, we must be confident the truth will emerge.

These fundamental guidelines, embodied in the First Amendment, apply to the march being debated today. The public is the final reservoir of thought, opinion and information. Let them judge theories, philosophies, and ideas based on all the evidence, not just on what is deemed acceptable.

(When all witnesses have spoken or when the time allotted for the forum is running out, the council president should call on the town legal counsel and then give a brief synopsis of each resolution. Hands should be counted in support and in opposition to each measure.)

PRESIDENT WHITCOMB: I believe I have called on all those who asked to be heard this evening. If we have no other witnesses from the audience, we will take a vote on the resolutions Councilman Mayer introduced. Once again, I remind you that these votes are not binding upon the council, and may in fact be mitigated by legal circumstances. Before we vote, I would like to ask Barry Newman, our legal counsel, to say a few words.

BARRY NEWMAN, LEGAL COUNSEL FOR LIBERTYVILLE: As legal counsel for Libertyville, I must inform you that the resolutions introduced today might face a very difficult battle against the First Amendment freedoms of speech and of assembly.

Courts have consistently declared that governmental bodies cannot regulate most speech if the restrictions are based on the content of the speech. Of course, there are some exceptions to that general rule, like obscene speech and print or political speech that advocates immediate violence. But, in general, political speech has the most constitutional protection of all forms of speech. Recent court cases dealing with Nazi propaganda in Skokie, Illinois, classified it as protected political speech.

As to one witness's contention that Nazi propaganda is obscene and can be regulated, I would say obtaining that kind of ruling would be a legal longshot. It's true some scholars have tried to classify similar speech as "group libel," supposedly without constitutional protection. But they base their argument on a 1954 precedent that hasn't been tested recently in court. If the council decides to try to outlaw this demonstration as "group libel," in my view, we would be in uncharted legal seas.

PRESIDENT WHITCOMB: Thank you, Mr. Newman, for that brief legal summary. I hope it has clarified some of the issues for both our observers and for council members.

First, we will vote on ordinance number *7001,* which outlaws any march by the Party of the American National Socialists, on April 20 or any other date. Those in favor please raise your hands. *(Count hands.)* Those opposed.

Next, we have ordinance number *7002,* which requires that any march or demonstration in Libertyville be accompanied by a city permit, issued 30 days in advance of the event, and by $1,500,000 in public liability and property damage insurance. Those in favor. *(Count hands.)* Those opposed.

Finally, we have ordinance number *7003,* which makes it unlawful for individuals or groups to engage in group libel against any sex, race, religion, or ethnic group. Those in favor. *(Count hands.)* Those opposed.

(The council president now reads the tallies for the three resolutions.)

Now we have some sense of community feeling on this subject. Once again, I want to thank you all for coming to this meeting to offer your ideas.

The council will now adjourn to consider the testimony given at this meeting and to consult with legal counsel.

Thank you.

(Participants playing "President Whitcomb" and other roles might now engage the audience in further socratic dialogue to elicit reactions to the issues presented and to develop discussion on the types of options and limitations Libertyville faces in reacting to the possibility of a violent demonstration.)

Memorandum on Legal Issues
Freedom of Assembly and Group Libel

Americans cherish their right to speak out on matters of importance to them, seeing this as one of the primary distinctions between a totalitarian state and one that allows its citizens to participate in their own governance. Freedom of various kinds of expression is guaranteed by the First Amendment to the U.S. Constitution.

The First Amendment not only guarantees to individuals the right to speak their mind, but it also guarantees groups the right to assemble peaceably in order to advocate certain doctrines or beliefs. That right has been an element of every major political movement in the United States from the Boston Tea Party, to the abolition of slavery, to winning a right to vote for women, to the modern civil rights movement. The Founding Fathers recognized the importance of freedom of assembly to the political life of the fledgling country, having sorely noted its absence during British colonial rule.

Freedom of political speech allows citizens to discuss possible alternatives to established public policy. Along with the attendant freedom of assembly, it has proved vital to the American democratic process throughout our history, providing a forum for individuals to speak and giving them the opportunity to ally with others who espouse beliefs similar to their own. These alliances—in effect, political parties—are cooperative efforts that provide strength in numbers. While one individual's speech may be limited by his access to the media or by his public stature, groups can garner more attention and exert more influence by their sheer numbers. Through this attention and influence, they may attract more followers and even be able to affect public policy.

Violence and the Right to Assemble

The only express limitation that the Constitution places on these gatherings is that they remain peaceful; when violence enters the picture the government's police power provides the basis for controlling the assembly. Still, in *New York Times v. Sullivan,* 376 U.S. 254, 270 (1964), the Supreme Court acknowledged discussion about issues of public moment must be "uninhibited, robust and wide-open, and that it may well include caustic and sometimes unpleasantly sharp attacks..."

A proposed Nazi march in Skokie, Illinois, brought the concept of freedom of assembly under close scrutiny in a 1977 case, in which the courts eventually upheld the marchers' right to demonstrate as constitutionally protected political speech.

The announcement that Nazis would march inflamed emotions in the Chicago suburb, noted for a large Jewish population that includes survivors of the Holocaust of World War II. The village of Skokie obtained an injunction to prohibit the planned march. Council members also drafted ordinances to prohibit similar demonstrations in the future. One required demonstrations on village streets be covered by a permit, issued at least 30 days in advance, and by insurance totaling $350,000. Permits would not be issued to demonstrators who incited negative reactions toward persons of specific religious, racial, ethnic, national or regional groups. Other ordinances prohibited literature defaming such groups and demonstrators who wore military-style uniforms on behalf of any political party.

The American Civil Liberties Union (ACLU) filed lawsuits in both state and federal courts on behalf of the sponsors of the march, the National Socialist Party of America. The first ACLU action, filed in Illinois state courts, successfully fought the injunction outlawing the Nazi march. An appellate court declared the march could take place, but only without the infamous swastika, equating the symbol of the Nazi party with "fighting words." *Village of Skokie v. National Socialist Party of America,* 51 Ill.App.3d 279 (1977), *rev'd,* 69 Ill.2d 605, 373 N.E.2d 21 (1978). "Fighting words," because they "tend to incite an immediate breach of peace," are considered outside the protection of the First Amendment. *Chaplinsky v. New Hampshire,* 315 U.S. 568, 572 (1942). The Supreme Court has even declared threats to the peace and security of a community can be controlled with censorship—a drastic measure otherwise reserved only for obscenity or damaging breaches in national security. *Near v. Minnesota,* 283 U.S. 697 (1931).

When the *Skokie* case was appealed, a 6-1 decision of the Illinois Supreme Court refused to say the swastika was an invitation to violence. According to the court:

> The display of the swastika, as offensive to the principles of a free nation or the memories it recalls may be, is symbolic political speech intended to convey to the public the beliefs of those who display it. It does not, in our opinion, fall within the doctrine of "fighting words," and that doctrine cannot be used here to overcome the heavy presumption against the constitutional validity of a prior restraint.
>
> *Skokie,* 373 N.E.2d at 24 (1978).

Defamation and Group Defamation

The second legal action filed by the ACLU, litigated in federal courts, sought to invalidate the village ordinances designed to prevent future marches by groups that preach hate. A federal district court declared various clauses in the Skokie ordinances violated the U.S. Constitution by being too vague and broad in scope. While Judge Bernard Decker acknowledged that publicly disseminating doctrines of racial and religious hatred could pose grave dangers, the alternative was even more threatening:

> When feelings and tensions are at their highest peak, it is a temptation to reach for the exception to the rule announced by Justice [Oliver Wendell] Holmes, "If there is any principle of the Constitution that more imperatively calls for attachment than any other it is the principle of free thought—not free thought for those who agree with us but freedom of the thought we hate." Freedom of thought carries with it the freedom to speak and to publicly assemble to express one's thoughts...when a choice must be made, it is better to allow those who preach racial hate to expend their venom in rhetoric rather than to be panicked into embarking on the dangerous course of the government to decide what its citizens must say and hear [citations omitted].
> *Collin v. Smith,* 447 F.Supp. 676, 702 (N.D.Ill. 1978).

Judge Decker's judgment was affirmed by the U.S. Court of Appeals, which declared:

> The National Socialist Party of America's beliefs and goals are repugnant to the core values held generally by residents of this country, and, indeed, to much of what we cherish in civilization. As judges sworn to defend the Constitution, however, we cannot decide this or any case on that basis. Ideological tyranny, no matter how worthy its motivation, is forbidden as much to appointed judges as to elected legislators.
> *Collin v. Smith,* 578 F.2d 1197, 1200 (7th Cir.), *cert. denied,* 436 U.S. 953 (1978).

When Illinois and federal courts refused to erect obstacles to the Skokie march, the state legislature proposed but did not pass a group defamation law as a means to approach the problem in another way. Because libel, like fighting words, is considered outside the First Amendment's protection, defamatory speech is subject to restriction. Group libel permits members of a large class of individuals to sue for defamation directed at the grouping as a whole. The courts have largely looked upon the concept with disfavor. Under common law, group libel was not actionable. *The King v. Alme & Nott,* 3 Salk. 224, 91 Eng.Rep. 790 (1699).

Interestingly, another Illinois case gave the Supreme Court an opportunity to examine group libel. In 1917, Illinois enacted a group defamation law that prohibited any publication which defamed citizens by casting aspersions on their race, color, creed, or religion. The Supreme Court, by a 5-4 vote, upheld the constitutionality of the law and the prosecution of a white supremacist in *Beauharnais v. Illinois,* 343 U.S. 250 (1952), though the validity of that ruling has been questioned in light of more recent decisions.

While the *Beauharnais* majority was slim, some scholars say even the dissenters indicated group libel laws could pass constitutional muster, if they were properly written and enforced. They objected to the wording of the Illinois statute, not to its intent.

If *Beauharnais* did not put group defamation outside of constitutional protection, others claim such speech should at least be an actionable tort, possibly for "intentional infliction of emotional distress." *See* K. Lasson, "Group Libel Versus Free Speech: When Big Brother *Should* Butt In," 23 Duq. L. Rev. 77-130, (Fall 1984).

Theory and Action

Since *Beauharnais* was handed down, however, the *Sullivan* decision made the First Amendment applicable to libel law. *Sullivan* and its progeny require that libel laws comport with certain requirements necessary to give meaning to the freedoms of speech and the press. Although *Sullivan* did not expressly overrule *Beauharnais*, it is difficult to imagine a rationale that allows the latter to remain good law. The Seventh Circuit in the *Collin* case "expressed doubt... that *Beauharnais* remains good law at all after the constitutional libel cases." 578 F.2d at 1205, *cert. denied,* 439 U.S. 916 (1978).

Beauharnais considered the potential for violent confrontation a factor in validating the Illinois group libel statute. However, restrictions on the content of speech are not permitted simply because the speech *might* tend to produce violence. Violence is only a factor permitting restriction if speech "is directed to inciting or producing imminent lawless action and is likely to incite or produce such action." *Brandenburg v. Ohio,* 395 U.S. 444, 447 (1969).

To be embraced by the "fighting words" doctrine and be outside of First Amendment protection, the Supreme Court has declared a dispute must involve face-to-face confrontations that insult listeners directly and do not just offend their sensibilities. On the basis of this distinction, the Court refused to allow authorities to prosecute someone who sported the words "fuck the draft" on his jacket in a county courthouse. *Cohen v. California,* 403 U.S. 15 (1971).

That "fighting words" must lead to an immediate breach of peace before speech loses its constitutional protection demonstrates a nuance in courts' interpretation of First Amendment freedoms: they clearly differentiate between espousing a *theory,* even if it might call for eventual overthrow of the government, and advocating immediate criminal *action.*

The distinction between theory and immediate action has not always been as defined as it is today. Its evolution began as the Supreme Court considered two free speech cases after the Bolshevik revolution in Russia led to a "red" scare. *Schenck v. United States,* 249 U.S. 47 (1919), and *Abrams v. United States,* 250 U.S. 616 (1919).

In *Schenck,* Justice Oliver Wendell Holmes wrote the majority opinion that resulted in the first American convictions for seditious speech since the Alien and Sedition Acts of 1798, punishing the appellants for mailing pamphlets criticizing the draft to those eligible for military service. Justice Holmes declared wartime conditions precluded extending First Amendment protection to speech that hindered the war effort, saying this was a "clear and present danger" akin to "falsely shouting fire in a theater." *Id.* at 52.

Holmes elaborated on the "clear and present danger" test in *Abrams,* this time in dissent. He wrote that criticizing American involvement in efforts to topple Russia's new communist government did not violate the Espionage Acts, as it did not "present danger of immediate evil or an intent to bring it about...Congress cannot forbid all effort to change the mind of the country." 250 U.S. at 628.

Holmes then penned what became one of the most famous passages in constitutional law:

> ...the best test of truth is the power of thought to get itself accepted in the competition of the market...That...is the theory of our Constitution...We should be eternally vigilant against attempts to check the expression of opinions we loathe and believe to be fraught with death, unless they so imminently threaten immediate interference with the lawful and pressing purposes of the law that an immediate check is required to save the country...Only the emergency that makes it immediately dangerous to leave the correction of evil counsels to time warrants making any exception to the sweeping command, "Congress shall make no law...abridging the freedom of speech."
> *Id.* at 630.

Courts continued to develop the "clear and present danger" test for political speech and assemblies through the early twentieth century. Some of these cases involved union organizers, who faced formidable opposition from those fearing the plans they advocated were dangerously close to communism. But in *Hague v. Committee for Industrial Organization,* 307 U.S. 496 (1939), the Supreme Court prohibited municipalities from excluding assemblies solely on the basis of a group's political philosophy. Streets and parks "have immemorially been held in trust for the use of the public and...have been used for purposes of assembly, communicating thought between citizens, and discussing public questions. Such use of the streets and public places has, from ancient times, been a part of the privileges, immunities, rights and liberties of citizens." *Id.* at 515-516.

Judicial interpretations of what met the test for "clear and present danger" fluctuated following World War II. In 1949, the Court upheld the free speech rights of a defrocked Catholic priest who denounced both Jews and blacks to a Chicago crowd. *Terminiello v. Chicago,* 337 U.S. 1 (1949). Writing for the Court, Justice William O. Douglas declared:

> A function of free speech under our system of government is to invite dispute. It may indeed best serve its high purpose when it induces a condition of unrest, creates dissatisfaction with conditions as they are, or even stirs people to anger. Speech is often provocative and challenging. It may strike at prejudice and preconceptions and have profound unsettling effects...That is why freedom of speech...is nevertheless protected against censorship or punishment, unless shown likely to produce a clear and present danger of a serious substantive evil that rises far about public inconvenience, annoyance, or unrest.
> *Id.* at 4.

But as the McCarthy era began, this line between speech and action was blurred in *Dennis v. United States,* 341 U.S. 494 (1951), a per curiam opinion that declared a conspiracy to advocate revolution, even if only in its planning stages, was a "clear and present danger." Thus, governmental authorities need not "wait until the putsch is about to be executed" before clamping down on such a conspiracy. *Id.* at 509. The Court retreated from this broad interpretation in *Yates v. United States,* 354 U.S. 298 (1957), saying restraints on freedom of expression were "aimed at the advocacy and teaching of concrete action for forcible overthrow of the Government, and not at principles divorced from action." *Id.* at 319-320.

The Court kept to this more generous guide during cases arising from the political protests and heightened awareness of the 1960s. In *Brandenburg v. Ohio,* 395 U.S. 444 (1969), the Court's per curiam opinion reversed the conviction of a Ku Klux Klan leader for violating a criminal syndicalism statute, declaring:

> [The state may not] forbid or proscribe advocacy of the use of force or of law violation except where such advocacy is directed to inciting or producing imminent lawless action and is likely to incite or produce such action.
> *Id.* at 447.

Content and Context

American courts have steered away from limiting freedom of assembly on the basis of *content,* as long as gatherings do not incite imminent lawless action. Courts are reluctant to condone such controls, since they open the door for government officials to censor those who espouse ideas alien to their own philosophy of government. In the worst possible scenario, limiting this freedom of expression could lead to totalitarian government, outlawing open gatherings of all groups regardless of their political or ideological stripe.

While content-related regulations are inherently suspect, "the privilege of a citizen of the United States to use the streets and parks for communication of views on national questions may be regulated in the interest of all,"

Hague v. CIO, 307 U.S. at 516. And, the concept of individual privacy permits even legitimate speech to be subject to reasonable time, place and manner restrictions. *Cox v. Louisiana,* 379 U.S. 536, 558 (1965).

Thus, the privilege implied in freedom of assembly is "not absolute, but relative, and must be exercised in subordination to the general comfort and convenience, and in consonance with peace and good order; but it must not, in the guise of regulation, be abridged or denied." *Hague, supra* at 516. Governmental units can then control the *context* of speech and assembly within the "public forum," as long as any restrictions are free of bias as to content. But "to be reasonable, time, place, and manner restrictions not only must serve significant state interests but also must leave open adequate alternative channels of communication." *Schad v. Borough of Mount Ephraim,* 452 U.S. 61, 68 (1981).

One way governments can regulate demonstrations and meetings within their environs is requiring groups obtain licenses for their gatherings. But, such licenses cannot require political demonstrators to take out liability insurance. This stipulation was declared unconstitutional in the district court's decision in the Skokie case, which held that an insurance requirement would unfairly discriminate against groups with limited financial resources and "impose a virtually insuperable obstacle to the free exercise of First Amendment rights in the Village of Skokie," *Collin v. Smith,* 447 F.Supp. at 685-686.

Even if would-be demonstrators dispute the way permits are awarded, if they ignore proper procedure in protest they can be punished:

> ...to allow applicants to proceed without the required permits to...hold public meetings without prior safety arrangements or take other unauthorized action is apt to cause breaches of the peace or create public dangers...Delay is unfortunate, but the expense and annoyance of litigation is a price citizens must pay for life in an orderly society where the rights of the First Amendment have real and abiding meaning.
> *Poulos v. New Hampshire,* 345 U.S. 395, 409 (1953).

Similarly, the proper way to combat what might be an unconstitutional restraining order is to appeal it, not to flagrantly violate the order. Under this reasoning, the Supreme Court upheld the conviction of Martin Luther King Jr. and other civil rights marchers when they violated an *ex parte* injunction instead of fighting it in court. In *Walker v. Birmingham,* 388 U.S. 307 (1967), the Court said:

> This Court cannot hold that the petitioners were constitutionally free to ignore all the procedures of the law and carry their battle to the streets. One may sympathize with the petitioners' impatient commitment to their cause. But respect for judicial process is a small price to pay for the civilizing hand of law, which alone can give abiding meaning to constitutional freedom.
> *Id.* at 321.

A later Court recognized demonstrators' difficulty in appealing *ex parte* injunctions such as that in *Walker,* since by definition they are issued without all parties being present. The Court held unconstitutional orders that restrain the holding of meetings or rallies if they are *ex parte,* without notice to the subjects of the order, and without at least an informal effort to invite the participation of all concerned. Such injunctions can be condoned only if those requesting the order prove it was impossible to notify the opposing parties. *Carroll v. President and Commissioners of Princess Anne,* 393 U.S. 175 (1968).

In addition to requiring demonstrators to be licensed, municipalities can limit the physical location of speech by statute if laws are narrowly drawn and unbiased about content. The Supreme Court first attempted to classify the "public forum" by physical location in *Perry Educational Association v. Perry Local Educators' Association,* 460 U.S. 37 (1983).

Writing the majority opinion in a 5-4 decision, Justice Byron White detailed three types of public forums, over which the state can exercise various degrees of control:

1. Those areas which have been public from time immemorial, such as streets or parks: to impose regulations there, governmental units must display a compelling state interest, regulatory statutes must be narrowly drawn and neutral about the content of speech;
2. Forums that the state has opened to public use, such as state universities: here, government cannot prohibit one group from advocating its ideas when it has allowed others to; and
3. Some sorts of public property may be reserved solely for the purpose they were originally intended: thus, government can forbid political demonstrations at military installations or in jails.

In the case of *Perry,* only the sanctioned teachers' union could be allowed use of faculty mailboxes.

Thus, under prevailing court opinion and precedent, narrow constraints may be imposed on the *context* of speech, as long as they do not discriminate on the *content* of speech. Regulations as to content are inherently suspect, even though some speech—like obscenity or libel—may be limited or punished. However, "group libel" does not qualify in this category, according to the most recent court ruling on the subject, but is instead defined as political speech.

NATIONAL SECURITY
AND THE PRESS

Publishing the Nation's Secrets

Cast of Characters, in order of their appearance

JUDGE MAVIS MITTELMAN
JOSEPH PERSHING, United States attorney
MATTHEW BOTICA, counsel for the defense
ALAN ARTHUR MCDURMOTT, United States Secretary of Defense
NADIA STANISLOWSKI, United States Air Force scientist
LARRY QUANTRAIN, columnist for the *Masses*
BRUCE ENDELMANN, former United States Air Force scientist

On August 8, the monthly *Masses* published a column by one of its regular contributors that detailed the workings of Mask, a highly technical system enabling planes and missiles to evade radar detection. Officials at the U.S. Department of Defense seized all copies of the edition containing the article and secured an injunction to stop its publication, saying it divulged classified military information. *Masses* countered the seizure and the injunction with a lawsuit, charging the government with unjustified prior restraint that violated the First Amendment of the U.S. Constitution.

While attorneys for the Defense Department and for *Masses* prepared for a courtroom showdown, another magazine, *The Guardian,* acquired a copy of the confiscated column from *Masses* and then published the original article in its entirety. *The Guardian* had editorially supported the claims of *Masses* to First Amendment protection, and it declared publishing the restricted article demonstrated that the press could not be muzzled. The issues of *The Guardian* containing the article, "Mask Sees Light of Day," were widely disseminated.

With the information that the government attempted to keep secret now indisputably in the public domain, both the pending lawsuit and the injunction were declared moot. Government officials decided to file criminal charges against the author of the Mask article and against the editors of both magazines, hoping to deter future breaches of national security in the press. Today, the charges against the reporter will be tried.

(This community forum takes place in federal court where Larry Quantrain, the author of "Mask Sees Light of Day," is charged with violating U.S. espionage laws. In the following mock trial, the audience will serve as jurors. Witnesses should face the audience when testifying.

A partial text of "Mask Sees Light of Day" appears below. Forum organizers should photocopy and distribute these excerpts so that the audience can refer to the article during the trial.)

The Masses

August 8, 19___

Mask Sees Light of Day

by Larry Quantrain

Our military establishment has been hit with science fiction fever lately. First, we have the "Star Wars" defense system to zap incoming missiles before they can threaten us, then we have "Stealth" and now we have "Mask." Mask's radar-evading technology was aptly named, although our movie-fan generals didn't realize how appropriate the moniker really is.

Mask's secret lies in its far-out and futuristic "cloaking device." It can dodge detection, allowing jets and missiles to make out-of-nowhere entrances and exits that surprise the enemy. But the real "secret" of Mask is that this mechanism only mimics the "fuzz busters" used by speed demons on every interstate in the country to avoid speeding tickets.

This analogy provides the basis for this analysis of Mask, a description drawn from research anyone can do. It was gleaned from U.S. Air Force magazines and employee brochures, from assembly-and-maintenance instructions for a radar jammer purchased at a local electronics store, from books, from articles, from interviews and from the logic of inference.

You might ask, "Why is he telling me this?" According to a sagacious journalism professor I once had, even if your mother tells you she loves you, you should check it out. Sometimes, questions have to be asked.

First off, I am not in this for the money. Anyone who can buy this issue is in on the secret. Second, I am not a commie dupe, deluded by Leninist-Marxist ideology and ready to sell out to the Ruskies. Third, I don't want some half-crazed terrorists to hold the United States hostage, although they might find this article helps advance their ends.

What I *am* trying to show by writing this article about Mask is that no scientific technology can remain "secret" for long. The secrecy surrounding Mask only allows the Pentagon to continue the arms race, to escalate the stockpiling that will bury us all. *This* is the insidious mask around Mask.

American defense strategists vaunt Mask as an Obi-Wan-Kenobi-like miracle that protects us against the Evil Empire. Like the heroes of *Star Wars*, those in command at the Pentagon believe they are morally anointed, chosen to win victory over the forces of oppression and tyranny.

As part of their Holy Crusade, the Defense Department has erected an aura of mystery, a circle of secrecy, around the Mask system. The Pentagon brass have become high priests in pagan rites, the sole initiates to a charmed circle of worldly power. They restricted information about Mask to the supposed chosen and to a selected few. By doing this, they convinced themselves, and unfortunately many Americans, that only an elite has the knowledge and wisdom to control powerful toys like Mask or nuclear armaments. But the confidentiality claimed for Mask is actually a cover-up.

This cover-up functions in two ways. It hides the usual cost overruns and mismanagement that accompany so many defense enterprises in this country. When the Department of Defense buys a weapon system, the sky literally is the limit. "Put on every option you can think of," they tell the defense contractors, "now where are we going to lunch? You can put that on my bill, too." The military-industrial complex is rife with such corruption: only Defense buys screwdrivers for thousands of dollars.

The second, and more scary, component of the cover-up is that it glosses over Defense's fallacious and grandiose claims about the "confidentiality" and "secrecy" of Mask. The truth?

The truth is that Mask is only a building block in the defense arsenal. It is not a panacea for any defense "problem."

The real "problem" is that the military-industrial movers and shakers see the world through a "we" and "they" prism: democratic capitalism versus authoritarian communism. Cut and dried. Black and white.

The "truth" is the "secrets" of Mask are common knowledge to anyone who has a rudimentary knowledge of the basic principles of mechanics and physics. They can be obtained easily by virtually anyone. By deluding ourselves into thinking we can censor scientific information, we allow the capitalistic, nationalistic arms race—the woe of the modern world—to continue. The only ones not aware of this secret are the American people, not the Siberian huskies the "top secret" stamp was invented for.

Does this make you a little uneasy? It should. You'll feel even less secure after finding out for yourself the "secrets" of Mask.

Before you continue, a caveat is in order. The proper "solution" to the Mask "problem" is not to relegate its secrets to a musty and mysterious realm inhabited only by scientists. What we should learn from this is that knowledge cannot be contained or kept from our "enemies." What we should learn from Mask is the importance of constant contact with other world powers, of working toward world peace.

(The remainder of the Masses *article contains detailed descriptions and drawings that explain the workings of the Mask system.)*

JUDGE MAVIS MITTELMAN: This court is now in session. Ladies and gentlemen of the jury, you have been selected to try the case of the United States versus Larry Quantrain, charged with violating the federal espionage laws. After you hear all of the evidence presented, I will instruct you on how to apply the law to reach a verdict. You have been sworn to consider only those facts presented before you in this court of law. If you have read or heard anything about this case, you are to try to put that out of your mind. The only facts you can consider are those you find credible from the testimony and exhibits presented today. You cannot discuss the testimony with anyone during the trial. I ask that you keep an open mind until you have heard all testimony, the attorneys' closing arguments, and my instructions on the law.

I do want to remind you that you are to treat each witness called in this case equally and to believe or disbelieve them as individuals. Hold them in no less or no more esteem simply because they hold public office or are figures in the community.

The prosecution may present its opening argument.

JOSEPH PERSHING, UNITED STATES ATTORNEY: Ladies and gentlemen of the jury, we live in a dangerous world, with thinly-veiled hostilities between countries and the ever-present threat of international terrorism. In such an uneasy world, the United States must have the capability to defend itself—to protect the precious liberties and rights guaranteed to all its citizens by our Constitution.

But the United States cannot protect itself if classified defense information is published, aiding our enemies and undermining the safety and security of the nation. This is just what the defendant did when he wrote a magazine column on the Mask security system.

As I will show through the course of this trial, the information used in that article was obtained and published in a way that violated the espionage laws of the United States. That article provided enough information to allow hostile interests to crack the Mask detection code and possibly circumvent its functioning. Through testimony, you will find that the article damaged U.S. security.

Thank you for your attention.

MATTHEW BOTICA, COUNSEL FOR THE DEFENDANT: Ladies and gentlemen of the jury. Today, you will be asked to consider two concepts that are crucial to the free and democratic society we know in the United States: the need for national security and freedom of the press.

First, the prosecution will try to show that Larry Quantrain revealed national secrets. He did not. The information in his column was found during research anyone could do. Certainly, hostile governments subscribe to the technical journals and other publications Mr. Quantrain used as sources. They did not wait for Mr. Quantrain to write his article, nor did it reveal anything they didn't already know.

Second, the prosecution will try to prove that the article damaged national security. This is also not so. Information easily available in the public realm and published in one place cannot undo a nation's security. Expert witnesses are available to testify to that.

Why then has this case been brought? Because the government fears those among us who dare to point out discrepancies in the official line, who forge ahead to more enlightened approaches—to hidden "truths"—in security issues, in social issues, in political issues. The kernels of such a truth were in the column at issue today. And by listening to the witnesses, you will see that Larry Quantrain is innocent of the charges of espionage brought against him. He had something to say, something worthy of our attention.

The claims of national security made for Mask in *no* way outweigh the need to protect the First Amendment freedoms of the press. In fact, the precedents of history show us what rare occasion we have to invoke "national security" over the right and freedom of the press to keep the populace informed.

You have the chance today to stand up for freedom. Listen to the testimony carefully, and you will see that this is the real issue today.

JUDGE MITTELMAN: The prosecution may begin its case.

PERSHING: I will call the government's first witness in this matter, Alan Arthur McDurmott. *(McDurmott is sworn under oath and takes the witness stand.)* Please state your name and occupation.

ALAN ARTHUR MCDURMOTT: I am Alan Arthur McDurmott, Secretary of Defense.

PERSHING: Mr. Secretary, are you familiar with what I am now handing to you?

MCDURMOTT: Yes, I am. It's a column called "Mask Sees Light of Day" that appeared in a magazine called *Masses* about a month ago. It was written by a reporter named Larry Quantrain.

PERSHING: I ask that the *Masses* column be marked Exhibit A. Mr. Secretary, what was your reaction to this article?

MCDURMOTT: I was *very* concerned, to put it mildly. That article detailed the functioning of one of our primary and most advanced weapons, communicating those secrets to anyone and everyone. The information it contained should have been suppressed; its disclosure jeopardized national security.

PERSHING: Mr. Secretary, what in particular was objectionable about "Mask Sees Light of Day?"

MCDURMOTT: It went far beyond discussing the demerits or merits of various weapons systems. The Department has no complaints with that sort of news coverage—it keeps our citizens reasonably well-informed of how their tax dollars are being spent.

We do our best at Defense to preserve the open system of government the Founders blessed us with. But the public cannot know *everything*—or our enemies will know it too. In such complicated and confidential matters, citizens have to trust their elected representatives, and the Department itself, to make decisions for them.

The *Masses* thought it knew better. It deliberately compromised Mask's confidentiality and published highly technical information, putting it within the reach of friend and foe alike. Worse yet, according to its author, the whole point of the article was to show the chinks in Mask's armor. It was an anti-military diatribe that sought to undermine our national security system.

PERSHING: Mr. Secretary, what happened after the Department of Defense learned of Mr. Quantrain's article?

MCDURMOTT: First, government attorneys asked for — and got — a temporary restraining order to prevent publication. *Masses* then filed a reply charging the order violated the First Amendment. While we were in the midst of that litigation, *The Guardian* published the original article. Unfortunately, we hadn't included *The Guardian* in the court order. At the time the order was issued, we didn't know they had the story. Anyway, after *The Guardian* article hit the newsstands, the court declared all litigation then filed moot.

PERSHING: In your opinion, Mr. Secretary, what would have been the proper action for *Masses* and *The Guardian* to take when they acquired the information in "Mask Sees Light of Day"?

MCDURMOTT: If they were responsible journalists, they would have contacted us, told us what they had and excised those portions we thought damaged our nation's security interests. Instead, they indulged in irresponsible journalism. The magazine staff knew it had struck a publicity-rich vein with the Mask story and went for the almighty dollar. They forgot about everything but their own interests.

PERSHING: Mr. Secretary, what effect did publication of the column have on the Mask project?

MCDURMOTT: It resulted in the waste of substantial research and development dollars. Supposedly, the column was trying to expose waste in the military budget. Instead, it damaged national security and wasted taxpayer dollars. The system as then developed was revealed. We had to return to the drawing board and change configurations to assure that Mask remains effective. While most of the damage done has been repaired, it can never be totally reversed. In our estimation, Mask will never again be as reliable a safety net as it was before.

PERSHING: Why is it important for the reporter in this case to be punished?

BOTICA: Objection, the witness is not qualified on the subject and the question asks the witness to argue a legal question.

JUDGE: Sustained.

PERSHING: Thank you, Mr. Secretary. Your witness.

BOTICA: Secretary McDurmott, isn't it true that much of the "classified" information in "Mask Sees Light of Day" was in fact already in the public domain?

MCDURMOTT: If the publication of certain information is detrimental to the national interest, it can be "classified" despite having appeared in what is technically the public domain. Besides, the public domain as defined in this case was a small circle of scientists. Scientific journals are a forum for "shop talk," not the wide audience Mr. Quantrain found with his article.

BOTICA: Mr. Secretary, who determines what is and what is not "classified"? And what exactly does "classified" mean?

MCDURMOTT: "Classified" information is divided into three groups by presidential order: "top secret" information is anything that could cause "exceptionally grave damage to the national security" if released; "secret" information could cause "serious damage" to national security if made public; and "confidential" information could cause "damage" to national security if released.

No set system exists for assigning these classifications, or for deciding who does the classifying. Presidents have usually given the secretaries of the various military branches the authority to mark anything "top secret." Their immediate subordinates determine what is kept "secret" or "confidential" and also who can access that information.

BOTICA: Isn't it true that more than *four million* people have access to classified materials at this time? How can you keep a secret when so many people are in on it?

MCDURMOTT: While I question the accuracy of your figures, we have initiated efforts to reduce the number of security clearances and to beef up the system. A task force was formed last month.

BOTICA: Mr. Secretary, let's go back to the question of "public domain." Are we to understand there are different degrees of the "public domain"? What appears in specialized scientific and trade journals is different from what can be published for general public consumption?

MCDURMOTT: There aren't different degrees. Public domain simply refers to making information commonly available. Terrorists don't read the scientific journals, but they do read *The New York Times* and probably even *Masses*.

BOTICA: But wasn't the information in Mr. Quantrain's article in *some* way available to anyone who knew where to look for it?

MCDURMOTT: That still doesn't mean he had to publish it. If Mr. Quantrain had considered the national security issues at stake, he would have thought a bit longer before he published.

BOTICA: No further questions.

PERSHING: The prosecution now calls Nadia Stanislowski. *(Stanislowski is sworn in.)* Please state your name and occupation for the record.

NADIA STANISLOWSKI: Nadia Stanislowski. I am a senior research and development scientist for the United States Air Force.

PERSHING: Dr. Stanislowski, how much knowledge do you have of the Mask system?

STANISLOWSKI: I am intimately acquainted with it. My graduate work at MIT laid the foundations for what became Mask. I later went to work for the Air Force full time, where Mask was developed.

PERSHING: In your opinion, Dr. Stanislowski, was the column "Mask Sees Light of Day" a fairly accurate portrayal of how Mask works?

STANISLOWSKI: Due to security considerations, I cannot answer your question in detail. But, it was accurate enough to pose a real threat to the health of our defense systems. We were forced to modify a number of Mask's frequency modulations.

PERSHING: How extensive was the damage to the Mask system?

STANISLOWSKI: We did what we could to limit the damage, but most repairs were stopgap or cosmetic surgery. Even so, the remedies were extensive. They involved constant backtracking, countless staff hours and numerous tax dollars. Any sort of punishment levied against the press could not *begin* to meet those expenses.

BOTICA: Objection.

JUDGE: Sustained. The jury will ignore that last remark from the witness.

PERSHING: In your opinion, Dr. Stanislowski, would you say the Mask article deliberately published state secrets about Mask, possibly for the consumption of those who could do harm to the United States?

BOTICA: Objection, the witness has no qualifications to answer that question. Any answer would be mere conjecture.

JUDGE: Sustained.

PERSHING: No further questions.

BOTICA: Dr. Stanislowski, I asked Secretary McDurmott earlier whether most of the information in "Mask Sees Light of Day" had previously appeared in scientific publications. You are a scientist. Don't you think Russian scientists read these publications and knew the information that *Masses* published?

STANISLOWSKI: I don't know whether Russian scientists read those journals or not. Even if they did, the journals only contained certain fragments of information. Long ago, the government determined it would be unproductive to censor scientific shoptalk. Scientists need a free flow of ideas to germinate new ones.

BOTICA: Would Russian scientists, if they had access to these journals, be capable of understanding and using the information about Mask technology?

STANISLOWSKI: I can't say for sure, but that is probably true.

BOTICA: Isn't it true that you don't even need much of a scientific background to understand what these journals had already printed?

STANISLOWSKI: I would disagree with that.

BOTICA: Then how do you explain that a layman like Larry Quantrain could obtain the information for his column from these journals?

STANISLOWSKI: I can't explain that.

BOTICA: Thank you.

PERSHING: The government rests its case, your honor.

JUDGE: Very well. Counsel for the defense may now present its case.

BOTICA: Your honor, I move that the charges against my client be dismissed for lack of evidence.

JUDGE: Motion denied.

BOTICA: The defense calls Larry Quantrain. *(Quantrain takes the stand and is sworn in.)* Please state your name and occupation.

LARRY QUANTRAIN: Larry Quantrain. I am a member of the Fourth Estate. That is, I'm a journalist.

BOTICA: Mr. Quantrain, you are the author of the column marked here as Exhibit A?

QUANTRAIN: Yup, that's my handiwork.

BOTICA: Where did you get the information for your column?

QUANTRAIN: I pieced together how Mask works by a process of simple deduction. Last winter I was out West on another assignment when I found an Air Force magazine with a short article on Mask. Anyway, after reading this article, I suddenly saw parallels between Mask's radar evasion capabilities and your basic "fuzzbuster." You see, I've always been an electronics buff on the side, and I've had a few college classes on the subject. From personal curiosity, I started researching a bit.

I went to the university library and the public library. All of my research is from documents found in libraries open to any Joe off the streets — and to secret agents too, I might add. Of course, some references to Mask in the literature were incomprehensible. I think these scientists could use a writing course. But, with what knowledge I had and what I got from other public sources, I was able to write my column.

BOTICA: Did you have any kind of security clearance for access to classified information to write "Mask Sees the Light of Day?"

QUANTRAIN: No, and I didn't need any. Anyone could have read it, and anyone with a basic knowledge of electronics could do exactly what I did if they had a little time and money to finance their research. Anyone: commies, quacks, terrorists — or just someone like me concerned about the level of defense expenditures. Speaking of which, all this makes me wonder why we are paying all these fancy scientific types so much if this is the best work they can do.

PERSHING: Objection.

JUDGE: Sustained. The witness will answer the questions and not add editorial comment.

BOTICA: Why did you write your column?

QUANTRAIN: The Defense Department claimed it had a "secret weapon." When a novice like me could pick up on the basics of that secret from easily available magazines, it seemed that Defense was trying to pull a fast one on the public. My job as a journalist is to watch out for and expose that sort of thing; that's why I wrote my column.

BOTICA: Do you believe you compromised national security?

QUANTRAIN: No, just the security of overpaid bureaucrats and Pentagon brass. I wanted to force people to think about how we throw money at defense, and I did it by showing them our weapons systems are not all that superior or all that secret. Puffing out our chests on misconceptions lulls us into a false sense of security.

I don't think we should accept everything we hear at face value. National security rests with each and every citizen, and we don't get it by pumping more and more money into so-called high-tech systems that you can buy at Radio Shack. We've all heard about wrenches and screwdrivers going for thousands of dollars.

BOTICA: Are you saying you wrote "Mask Sees Light of Day" without intending to undermine the national security of the United States?

QUANTRAIN: On the contrary, I believe what I did was an act of patriotism. In order to make the United States a truly functioning and progressive democracy, we need an informed and knowledgeable citizenry. We can't believe and support *everything* we are told.

I feel my article was much-needed and thoughtful criticism of a public policy gone awry.

BOTICA: Your witness.

PERSHING: Mr. Quantrain, what qualifications do you have to decide what is in the best interests of the country?

QUANTRAIN: "The best interests of the country" obviously means different things to different people. But that's the beauty of the First Amendment, we all have a legitimate right to our opinion, and a legitimate right to tell others about that opinion. If we have the facts, which is what I tried to do, we can each decide for ourselves what those best interests are.

PERSHING: Did you at any time conspire with those *inside* the government to procure classified information?

QUANTRAIN: No, and I stopped beating my wife last March. I commited no crime. As I've said before, my primary sources were all in the public domain. I did not "conspire" with anyone to do anything. However, I did receive specific confirmations from a source once connected with the project.

PERSHING: Mr. Quantrain, did you realize such activity could result in criminal actions against both you and your source?

QUANTRAIN: We committed no crime.

PERSHING: Did you know that even information in the so-called public domain may still be classified?

QUANTRAIN: Well, then I would say the task force assigned to redefine "classified" has its work cut out for it. How can something be both classified and available in the public domain? That's ludicrous.

PERSHING: Thank you, Mr. Quantrain. No further questions.

BOTICA: The defense now calls Dr. Bruce Endelmann to the stand. *(Endelmann is sworn in.)* State your name and occupation.

BRUCE ENDELMANN: I am Dr. Bruce Endelmann, professor of advanced engineering at Western Technical Institute.

BOTICA: Dr. Endelmann, what connection do you have to Mask?

ENDELMANN: Dr. Stanislowski and I were colleagues at the inception of the research that led to Mask. Unlike Dr. Stanislowski, however, I became more and more disenchanted with my work with the government defense apparatus. I left my government post three years ago.

BOTICA: Doctor, in the three years since you left the government's employ, have you ever been questioned about your involvement in Mask?

ENDELMANN: Only once.

BOTICA: By whom?

ENDELMANN: Larry Quantrain.

BOTICA: Dr. Endelmann, how did you become acquainted with Larry Quantrain?

ENDELMANN: I met Mr. Quantrain when he was writing an article on medical technology. We talked at length, and he learned I had worked for the Department of Defense at one time. At that time, he only asked general questions about my work, although he had a firm sense of what projects I worked on.

BOTICA: Dr. Endelmann, when did you find out that Mr. Quantrain was researching an article on Mask?

ENDELMANN: Not until he called me right before the article went to press. He explained he had obtained all of his information from public data, but he wanted to make sure he understood some of the details. As he told me what he knew or surmised, I was amazed. His conception of Mask suffered from only minor errors of omission and detail.

BOTICA: Did you tell him about those errors?

ENDELMANN: Not exactly. I told him to run the article as was, because it would shake up enough people in the right way. I think he understood that statement to mean the article had a few minor holes. I did not inform him about what was omitted. That information was classified.

BOTICA: Can you tell us about those errors now?

ENDELMANN: No, that information remains classified.

BOTICA: You said you were disillusioned working for the defense establishment. Did it have anything to do with the Mask project?

ENDELMANN: Mask was a perfect example of what was bothering me. I realized the secrecy about Mask was just another misconception. Some of the bureaucrats at Defense tried to persuade themselves and the American people that it was absolute protection. Amazingly, those who technically know the least about such systems often have the most faith in their infallibility. They think we can control scientific knowledge by cornering the market.

BOTICA: In your professional opinion, did Mr. Quantrain's article compromise national security?

ENDELMANN: No, it did not. The information was available to anyone, including those enemies who are the most likely to search for it.

BOTICA: Thank you, Doctor. Your witness.

PERSHING: I have no questions for this witness.

JUDGE: Does the defense have any further witnesses?

BOTICA: No, your honor. The defense rests its case.

JUDGE: Then we are ready for counsels' closing arguments. Mr. Pershing.

PERSHING: Ladies and gentlemen of the jury, history illuminates the important task before you as you decide the guilt or innocence of journalist Larry Quantrain.

Since the turn of the century, the United States has emerged as a great power, a democratic order that can both protect itself and help foster a better world for others. According to many historians, today's world was born in the trenches of World War I. The Great War began an era of rapid change in all aspects of life: from the munitions used to fight wars to the communications used to report them.

Technology has made communications an immediate and pervasive part of our lives. Because of our traditions of free speech and a free press, the United States has become the most advanced information society on earth. Most of today's conveniences have made life easier. But modernization has not missed any field of endeavor: war can now be waged with a destructiveness unimaginable to our ancestors. Since the birth of the machine gun shortly before World War I, the technology and sophistication of weaponry has advanced exponentially. To protect our cherished freedoms, we have to preserve a position of parity with those who might harm us.

In America, national security and freedom of the press maintain a working truce. We protect our security as best we can without causing unnecessary harm to the values of openness we all share. But sometimes freedom of the press *must* yield before national security. The case before you, the case of Mask and Larry Quantrain, is such an instance.

You have heard testimony from the highest defense official in the land, the man who, after the President, is responsible for assuring our security. He has told you how defense secrets were revealed by a sensationalism that Larry Quantrain claims as journalism. By detailing the workings of Mask, the defendant seriously damaged our ability to protect both America and our allies in Western Europe. Mr. Quantrain himself told you he did this knowingly and willingly. Judge Mittelman will soon explain the espionage law to you. Mr. Quantrain violated that law.

Larry Quantrain's counsel will try to tell you this case involves freedom of the press. Freedom of the press is a true hallmark of our democratic society, but it must yield when the security of our country is at stake.

This is why I now ask you to return a verdict of guilty. Thank you.

JUDGE: Mr. Botica.

BOTICA: Ladies and gentlemen of the jury, I commend you for your patience in this complicated and technical case. Now you must weigh the evidence you have heard in this courtroom. The prosecuting attorney is right when he says your decision requires you to weigh the freedom of the press with national security. However, he makes the national security interest in this case to be more than it really is.

You heard how all the information that was published was easily available in university and public libraries. Certainly, foreign enemies didn't wait for Larry Quantrain to investigate the Mask system. They know which journals publish that type of information, and they subscribe to them. Ask yourself: if this information is easily available even though it's classified, why are the author and editors of this articles being prosecuted?

The reason, the testimony makes evident, is that they didn't focus solely on the waste and fraud the defense establishment has inflicted on the American people. They published an article on a supposedly "forbidden" topic, something the Department of Defense could try to nail them with. I hope you will take to heart the testimony of Larry Quantrain. He published "Mask Sees Light of Day" because of—not in spite of—his love of the freedoms of this country. Government counsel does him a terrible disservice by implying otherwise. The action filed against Larry Quantrain obscures what is really at issue: the fact that Mask is *not* secret and not infallible. National security is a screen to hide what the Department of Defense does not want to face up to. And Mr. Quantrain's column exposed that.

Larry Quantrain believed the American people deserved a full airing of the claims made for Mask. He knew when he wrote his column that it might upset the military establishment. But he took the First Amendment seriously and believed in his obligation to keep the American people informed about how their tax dollars are being spent.

Because he told no secrets, Larry Quantrain cannot be punished for espionage. You will remember the famous "Pentagon Papers" case. *The New York Times* and later *The Washington Post* published non-technical, yet politically controversial, material on American military involvement in Vietnam. They were classified "top secret-sensitive," but the Supreme Court, by an overwhelming 6-3 vote, declared the *Times* could continue publication. The military was trying to cover up an embarrassing episode. In the case before us today, the military is once again hiding behind national security instead of owning up to the snafu it created.

What we have to realize here is that Larry Quantrain was only doing the legwork for the rest of us. By publishing "Mask Sees Light of Day," he and

Masses were exercising the right of political speech for all Americans. By rendering a verdict of not guilty today, you will strike a blow for liberty.

Thank you.

JUDGE: Ladies and gentlemen of the jury, this concludes the formal testimony and presentations of this trial. It now becomes my duty to give you the instructions of the court concerning the law applicable to this case.

It is your duty as jurors to follow the law as I shall state it to you, and to apply that law to the facts as you find them from the evidence in the case. You are not to single out one instruction alone as stating the law, but must consider the instructions as a whole. Neither are you to be concerned with the wisdom of any rule of law that I should state.

Your verdict must represent the considered judgment of each juror. In order to return a verdict, each juror must agree. In other words, your verdict must be unanimous.

It is your duty as jurors to consult with one another and to deliberate with a view to reaching an agreement, if you can do so without violence to individual judgment. Each of you must decide the case for yourself, but only after an impartial consideration of all the evidence in the case with your fellow jurors. In the course of your deliberations, do not hesitate to re-examine your own views and change your opinion, if you become convinced it is erroneous. But do not surrender your honest conviction as to the weight or effect of the evidence, solely because of the opinion of your fellow jurors, or for the mere purpose of returning a verdict.

Remember at all times you are not partisans. You are judges — judges of the facts. Your sole interest is to seek the truth from the evidence in the case.

Now, I have said that you must consider all of the evidence. This does not mean, however, that you must accept all evidence as true or accurate.

You are the sole judges of the credibility or "believability" of each witness. You should consider his or her relationship to the prosecution or to the defendant; his candor, fairness and intelligence; and the extent to which he has been supported or contradicted by other credible evidence. You may, in short, accept or reject the testimony of any witness in whole or in part.

Also, the weight of the evidence is not necessarily determined by the number of witnesses testifying as to the existence or non-existence of any fact. You may find that the testimony of a smaller number of witnesses as to any fact is more credible than the testimony of a larger number of witnesses to the contrary.

The defendant in this case has been charged with several criminal violations:

- "Gathering, transmitting or losing defense information" with the "intent or reason to believe" that the information would be used to the injury of the United States, or to the advantage of any foreign nation;

- "unauthorized" possession of, access to, or control over any material relating to the national defense which could be used in a similar manner; and
- disclosure of classified information, "specifically designated by a U.S. government agency for limited or restricted dissemination or distribution."

If you find the defendant has engaged in any one of these activities, you are to find him guilty. As judges of the facts, you may decide for yourselves whether the information disclosed was related to security concerns. It is not a crime, however, to disclose information already in the public domain, except in the case of nuclear weaponry and technology. But, even if information has previously been released, the government can determine whether further release will harm national interests. Your own conscience should guide you on this question.

The jury may now begin its deliberations as to whether Mr. Quantrain's article violated the law.

(The judge now leads a discussion for the jury's deliberations, with the audience serving as jurors. After all who offer an opinion have spoken or when time is running out, the judge polls participants for votes on each of the three charges leveled against Larry Quantrain.)

Memorandum on Legal Issues

National Security and the Press

Within the framework of the U.S. Constitution, American law weighs the dictates of national defense with the freedom of expression guaranteed by the First Amendment. Because national security is a prerequisite to preserving the system that supports our civil liberties, even censorship has been justified to maintain it; such a drastic measure of control is prohibited to nearly every other area of public expression, except obscenity and "fighting words."

One category of technology related to defense, nuclear science, has always been demarcated "top secret" and subject to impressive security restraints. In fact, only in this one area has Congress explicitly legislated a very narrow authorization for prior restraints on freedom of expression, allowing the executive branch to secure an injunction against criminal provisions of the Atomic Energy Act.

The *Progressive* Case

Such an injunction was obtained against a 1979 article in *The Progressive* called "The H-bomb Secret: How We Got It — Why We're Telling It." The author and editors of "The H-Bomb Secret" said the information they published was truly not a secret; they wanted to publish it to make a statement about the proliferation of nuclear weapons and know-how.

A temporary restraining order was issued to bar publication of the article and the U.S. Department of Energy initiated a legal action under the Atomic Energy Act, 42 U.S. Code Sec. 2011, *et seq.* The Act prohibits individuals with "access to...any document, writing, sketch, photograph, plan, model, instrument, appliance, note or information involving or incorporating Restricted Data" from revealing it "with intent to [or reason to believe it will] injure the United States or...secure an advantage to any foreign nation." Criminal penalties, upon conviction, are imprisonment for life; imprisonment for any term of years or a fine of not more than $20,000; or both. 42 U.S.C. Sec. 2274. The Act also authorizes an injunction to prevent secrets from being revealed.

The Atomic Energy Act, first enacted at the dawn of the nuclear age as the Cold War began, indefinitely extended certain controls on the production of and information about nuclear weaponry. According to *The Progressive,* the Act was obsolete, because knowledge about nuclear energy and weaponry no longer belongs to an exclusive club of countries. In fact, the magazine contended all information in the story on the H-bomb was gleaned from "public" sources: from declassified documents the government slipped onto public shelves at Los Alamos Scientific Library in New Mexico; and from articles in the *Milwaukee Sentinel, Fusion* magazine, and the *Encyclopedia Americana.*

In *United States v. The Progressive, Inc.,* 486 F.Supp. 5 (D.Wis.1979), the magazine asked a federal court to vacate the restraining order filed against it, charging the government with censorship in violation of its First Amendment free expression rights.

The court found that the government did not automatically move two documents into the public domain by inadvertently declassifying them; that "radiation coupling" and two other key concepts included in the *Progressive* article had not appeared in the public domain; and that publication or disclosure of the restricted data included in the article would likely violate the Atomic Energy Act, causing direct, immediate and irreparable injury to the nation.

According to government attorneys' arguments, which the judge found persuasive, other publications on the same topics were mere "literature of speculation," "so speculative and disjointed as to be meaningless." Further, the judge found circumstances surrounding the H-bomb article differed from conditions present in a case eight years earlier, when *The New York Times* published a series on American involvement in Vietnam:

> The government states that, unlike the situation in the Pentagon Papers case, no other publications have published the same or similarly accurate, comprehensive and detailed articles on the construction of hydrogen weapons. Thus the preliminary injunction against the defendants would still be effective and is warranted under the provisions of 42 U.S.C. Section 2230. The government argues that, even in the absence of this statutory authority, the injunction would still be warranted because of the existence of the likelihood of direct, immediate and irreparable injury to this country.
>
> *Progressive,* 486 F.Supp. at 7.

The district judge then declared that even if the government has already released information or a document, such a release is not binding if further disclosure is seen as detrimental. See also, *Aspin v. Department of Defense,* 453 F. Supp. 520 (E.D. Wisc. 1978); *Halperin v. CIA,* 446 F.Supp. 661 (D.D.C. 1978).

Eventually, the "public" nature of the information in *The Progressive* article resulted in a somewhat inconclusive victory for the press. As the case continued in the U.S. Court of Appeals, another newspaper published a reader's letter including much of the technical information in the restricted article. Since the U.S. government's action thus tried to stop publication of information now on newsstands, the litigation was moot, and the court proceedings were dropped.

Concerns about national security which came to the fore in *The Progressive* case did not cause a bipolar rift between journalists and government, although the Wisconsin-based magazine and its do-it-yourself guide to "The Bomb" became a hot topic for those in and out of journalism. The legal problems of the magazine focused attention on both nuclear weaponry and on whether—or how much—a publication can be subjected to prior restraint to protect national security.

Prior Restraints and National Security

The propriety of using prior restraints on the press to defend national security was condoned by *Near v. Minnesota,* 283 U.S. 697 (1931), a case otherwise declaring censorship of publications was inherently suspect as a severe infringement on First Amendment freedoms. In *Near,* a 5-4 Supreme Court lifted an injunction barring publication of an anti-Semitic newspaper, judging censorship to be an extreme reaction to counter its charges.

Although the majority barred further restraints on Jay Near's *The Saturday Press,* it did note three instances where censorship might be justified: to protect national security; to outlaw obscene publications; and to prevent violence and the forceful overthrow of the government. The *Near* majority opinion, authored by Chief Justice Charles Evans Hughes, was written with an eye to the technology of its own day:

> ...the protection even as to previous restraint is not absolutely unlimited. But the limitation has been recognized only in exceptional cases: "When a nation is at war many things that might be said in time of peace are such a hindrance to its effort that their utterance will not be endured so long as men fight and that no court could regard them as protected by any constitutional right," *Schenck v. United States,* 249 U.S. 47, 52 (1919). No one would question but that a government might prevent actual obstruction to its recruiting service or the publication of the sailing dates of transports or the number and location of troops.
>
> *Id.* at 716.

Forty years later, the Supreme Court pointed to *Near*'s prohibitions against prior restraint in *New York Times v. the United States,* 403 U.S. 713 (1971), ruling even the national security considerations then claimed did not justify a ban on publication of the "Pentagon Papers."

The Pentagon Papers were a classified, multi-volume study of U.S. involvement in Vietnam, leaked by a former government employee disillusioned with American policy there. They did not contain any technical data on weapons or electronics or any information on intelligence agents still in the field—all of which could have jeopardized then-current U.S. interests.

While nothing in the Pentagon Papers was immediately damning to national security, the Nixon Administration sought to stop their publication, believing what they revealed would further fuel the fury of anti-war protesters and American opposition to the war.

The Administration brought a civil suit to enjoin publication in both *The New York Times* and *The Washington Post*. Given the prominence and importance of the actors and issues involved, just 17 days later the Supreme Court ruled on the case, filing nine separate opinions. Two justices enunciated an "absolutist" position on First Amendment freedoms for the press, declaring that prior restraint was *never* justified.

Four justices, a possible "swing" vote in future questions of press freedom and national security, said prior restraint might be admissible in some circumstances, but not in the Pentagon Papers instance. Justice William Brennan's concurrence touched upon the relatively narrow conditions in which prior restraint would be admissible, all of which were subject to judicial review:

> ...only governmental allegation and proof that publication must inevitably, directly, and immediately cause the occurrence of an event kindred to imperiling the safety of a transport already at sea can support even the issuance of an interim restraining order. In no event may mere conclusions be sufficient: for if the Executive Branch seeks judicial aid in preventing publication, it must inevitably submit the basis upon which that aid is sought to scrutiny by the judiciary.
> *Id.* at 726-727.

In Justice Byron White's concurrence, joined by Justice Potter Stewart, he noted the government could take other action against unauthorized disclosure:

> Prior restraints require an unusually heavy justification under the First Amendment; but failure by the Government to justify prior restraint does not measure its constitutional entitlement to a conviction for criminal publication. That the Government mistakenly chose to proceed by injunction does not mean that it could not successfully proceed in another way.
> *Id.* at 733.

The dissenting three justices would have at least temporarily restrained publication of the Pentagon Papers, holding the hastiness with which the case was brought before the Court precluded consideration of a number of important issues — issues like defense classifications, the implications of *Near* on national security considerations, and the espionage statutes themselves. In his dissent, Justice Harry Blackmun complained the competing issues at stake had not been properly weighed:

> The First Amendment, after all, is only one part of an entire Constitution. Article II of the great document vests in the Executive Branch primary power over the conduct of foreign affairs and places in that branch the responsibility for the Nation's safety. Each provision of the Constitution is important, and I cannot subscribe to a doctrine of unlimited absolutism for the First

Amendment at the cost of downgrading other provisions. First Amendment absolutism has never commanded a majority of this Court.
Id. at 761.

Blackmun then cited the passage from *Schenck* that Chief Justice Hughes noted in *Near,* concluding that:

> What is needed here is a weighing, upon properly developed standards, of the broad right of the press to print and the very narrow right of the Government to prevent. Such standards are not yet developed. The parties here are in disagreement as to what those standards should be. But even the newspapers concede that there are situations where restraint is in order and is constitutional. Justice Holmes gave us a suggestions when he said in *Schenck,* at 52: "It is a question of proximity and degree."
> *Id.*

Basically, the justices followed the 40-year-old reasoning of *Near,* declaring the First Amendment carries a heavy constitutional burden against prior restraint that requires the government to have ample proof to justify such actions. The Court also clearly stated that considerations about the constitutionality of such restraints should not rest solely with the executive branch.

Some media watchers and talkers hailed *New York Times* as a wondrous victory, but others pointed out it was decided only on the specific facts concerning publication of the Pentagon Papers. According to authors Harvey Zuckman and Martin Gaynes:

> ...what appeared at first blush to be a great victory for the press is, at best, a pyrrhic one. The Court has given notice that there are limits to the media's right to publish and the people's right to learn government secrets relating to national security. As a result of this case, the media may become more wary of publishing classified materials obtained without authorization. At best the Pentagon Papers case encourages self censorship by the news media and at worst forms the predicate for successful government censorship in the future.
> *Mass Communications Law,* (St. Paul, Minn.: West Publishing Company, 1983).

Executive Privilege

In lower court actions concerning the Pentagon Papers, the government based its case against publication on the espionage statutes included in the U.S. Code. But by the time the case reached the Supreme Court, government attorneys were resting their argument on the inherent powers of the President. Historically, courts have given the strictest possible scrutiny to any unilateral executive action that attempts to restrain the civil liberties of citizens, but they have also recognized that occupants of the presidential office have privileged information about certain subjects that gives them a special perspective.

A mere three years after it ruled on the Pentagon Papers case, the Court explicitly recognized this "executive privilege" in *United States v. Nixon,*

418 U.S. 683 (1974). Writing the opinion for a unanimous Court, Chief Justice Warren Burger declared that:

> The expectation of a President to the confidentiality of his conversations and correspondence, like the claim of confidentiality of judicial deliberations, for example, has all the values to which we accord deference for the privacy of all citizens and, added to those values, is the necessity for protection of the public interest in candid, objective and even blunt or harsh opinions in Presidential decision-making. A President and those who assist him must be free to explore alternatives in the process of shaping policies and making decisions and to do so in a way many would be unwilling to express except privately. These are the considerations justifying a presumptive privilege for Presidential communications. The privilege is fundamental to the operation of Government and inextricably rooted in the separation of powers of the Constitution. In *Nixon v. Sirica,* 487 F.2d 700, 717 (D.C.Cir. 1973), the Court of Appeals held that such Presidential communications are "presumptively privileged," and this position is accepted by both parties in the present litigation.
>
> *Id.* at 708.

The "present litigation" involved a claim to executive privilege by President Richard Nixon, who had tried to quash a subpoena demanding tapes of possibly incriminating conversations recorded in the Oval Office. The tapes were subpoenaed in connection with criminal proceedings against the Watergate defendants, on trial for "burglarizing" Democratic National Headquarters on behalf of the Committee to Re-Elect the President.

The Supreme Court, with Justice William Rehnquist excused as a former Nixon Justice Department official, declared the president had to give up the tapes to ensure due process of law for the criminal defendants. But, as in *New York Times v. United States,* Chief Justice Burger based his opinion on the specific facts of the case, noting legitimate reasons could exist to invoke executive privilege, particularly for considerations of national security:

> In this case, the President challenges a subpoena served on him as a third party requiring the production of materials for use in a criminal prosecution; he does so on the claim that he has a privilege against disclosure of confidential communications. He does not place his claim of privilege on the ground they are military or diplomatic secrets. As to these areas of Article II duties the courts have traditionally shown the utmost deference to Presidential responsibilities.
>
> *Nixon, supra* at 710.

Given the reasoning underlying both *New York Times v. United States* and *United States v. Nixon,* governmental authorities might well conclude that courts have signaled that censorship can be condoned for security reasons. At the time *New York Times* was decided, the Nixon Administration took another tack in attempting to punish publication of the Pentagon Papers. It decided to criminally prosecute former government employee Daniel Ellsberg, as well as Anthony Russo, both then working at the Rand Corporation, who leaked the information published as the papers. Their trial failed to conclusively resolve the questions it raised, since it was dismissed when government prosecutors overstepped propriety with investigations into Ellsberg's psychiatric history. [The text of Judge Matthew Byrne's oral opinion in Ellsberg's trial is reprinted in the House Judiciary Committee Impeachment Inquiry: *Hearings on House Resolution 803, Statement of Information,* 93d Cong., 2d Sess., Book VII, part 4, at 2076 (1974).]

As filed, the criminal charges against Ellsberg and Russo rested on relevant sections of the U.S. Code dealing with espionage and censorship, Title 18 U.S. Code, Chapter 37, sections 793-798. The various sections classified certain activities as espionage: Section 792, "harboring or concealing persons;" Section 793, "gathering, transmitting or losing defense information;" Section 794, "gathering or delivering defense information to aid a foreign government;" Section 795, "photographing and sketching defense installations;" Section 796, "use of aircraft for photographing defense installations;" Section 797, "publication and sale of photographs of defense installations;" Section 798, "disclosure of classified information;" Section 799, "violation of regulations of National Aeronautics and Space Administration." The defendants were charged with violating sections 793 and 798 of the Code.

Besides referring to relevant sections of the U.S. Code, government attorneys in the Ellsberg and Russo case relied on court precedents about the constitutional issues involved in disclosing information sensitive to national security.

Cases Relating to the Espionage Acts

In *Gorin v. United States,* 312 U.S. 19 (1941), the Court declared "relating to the national defense," the language used in the U.S. Code, was not too broad or vague to be constitutional, but "a generic concept of broad connotations referring to the military and naval establishments and the related activities of national preparedness." *Id.* at 28. But this phraseology alone was not sufficient: "The obvious delimiting words in the statute are those requiring 'intent or reason to believe that the information to be obtained is to be used to the injury of the United States, or to the advantage of any foreign nation.' This requires those prosecuted to have acted in bad faith. The sanctions apply only when *scienter* is established." *Id.* at 27-28. Finally, *Gorin* stipulated: "The question of the connection of the information with national defense is a question of fact to be determined by the jury..." *Id.* at 32.

In *United States v. Heine,* 151 F.2d 813 (2d Cir. 1945), *cert. denied,* 328 U.S. 833 (1946), an appeals court declared gathering information *entirely* from public sources is not a crime. Under this ruling, a German-American citizen who collected information about U.S. airplanes did not violate the Espionage Act, although he was prosecuted for failing to file as an agent of a foreign government. While Heine misrepresented his motives for gathering the information, which he intended to pass to Germany in the event of war, Judge Learned Hand declared:

> All of this information came from sources that were lawfully accessible to anyone who was willing to take the pains to find, sift, and collate it; no public authorities, naval, military or other, had ordered, or indeed suggested, that the manufacturers of airplanes — even including those made for the services — should withhold any facts which they were personally willing to give out.
>
> *Id.* at 815.

In *Scarbeck v. United States,* 317 F.2d 546 (D.C. Cir. 1963), *cert. denied,* 374 U.S. 856 (1963), the District of Columbia Circuit Court declared government officials other than the President were empowered to classify documents and information. In addition, juries could only consider whether a document was classified, not whether it should have been:

> We conclude that it is the intent of the statute to make the superior's classification binding on the employee...The factual determination required for purposes of Section 783(b) is whether the information has been classified and whether the employee knew or had reason to know it was classified. Neither the employee nor the jury is permitted to ignore the classification given under Presidential authority.
>
> *Id.* at 560.

Gorin, Heine and *Scarbeck* settled some issues of statutory interpretation and constitutional law. Others surfaced during Daniel Ellsberg's trial, including those concerning the definition of "unauthorized possession" and "not entitled to receive," included in the U.S. Code. These ambiguities were temporarily submerged when the Ellsberg trial was dismissed.

Since the civil and criminal litigation involving the Pentagon Papers, courts have considered other cases dealing with national security and freedom of expression. A number focused on former government employees who wanted to publish writings based on their experiences in security-sensitive areas.

Prepublication Review

In *United States v. Marchetti,* 466 F.2d 1309 (4th Cir.), *cert. denied,* 409 U.S. 1063 (1972), the Court of Appeals declared a former Central Intelligence Agency employee, who wanted to publish a memoir of his years with the agency, was bound by a security agreement signed upon employment. The agreement stated writings were to be submitted to a prepublication review to prevent the revelation of classified information. Declaring the agreement pertained only to classified information, the court ruled it did not violate the defendant's First Amendment rights, as he had argued. However, the three judges presiding in the case could not agree whether the classification system itself was subject to judicial review.

The appellate court's ruling in *Marchetti* started a second round of proceedings, as he and his publisher wrangled with the government over what was classified, *Alfred A. Knopf, Inc. v. Colby,* 509 F.2d 1362 (4th Cir.), *cert. denied,* 421 U.S. 992 (1975). The CIA originally wanted to delete 399 items from Marchetti's book, *The CIA and the Cult of Intelligence,* co-authored with a former employee of the State Department, John Marks. After negotiations, the number of allegedly classified items marked for deletion was pared to 168.

According to the plaintiffs and their counsel, classification procedures are designed to control the dissemination and storage of documents, not to comment on the classification status of all information included in those documents. For example, each page of a document may be stamped "classified," but only a small number of sentences would actually include information which would be detrimental to the national defense if published. Following this reasoning, Marchetti, Marks and their publisher wanted the court to rule on the propriety of the classifications assigned to the items in dispute.

The same judges who ruled in *Marchetti* presided over *Knopf,* declaring once again that Marchetti had waived his First Amendment rights in reference to classified information when he signed the CIA security agreement. The judges determined information is not in the public domain unless it is officially disclosed; that a government official may not leak information and then claim it exists in the public domain; and that a former government employee may not publish information he first learned of in a confidential setting:

> Rumor and speculations circulate and sometimes get into print. It is one thing for a reporter or author to speculate or guess that a thing may be so or even, quoting undisclosed sources, to say that it is so; it is quite another thing for one in a position to know of it officially to say that it is so. The reading public is accustomed to treating reports from uncertain sources as being of uncertain reliability, but it would not be inclined to discredit reports of sensitive information revealed by an official of the United States in a position to know of what he spoke.
>
> *Id.* at 1370.

Although the appellate court's decision basically went against Marchetti, it did recognize amendments made to the Freedom of Information Act (FOIA) in 1974 had "introduced new considerations" to the case.

The Freedom of Information Act, included in the United States Code, allows any citizen to contest the propriety of a document's classification to compel its release. Pub. L. No. 93-502, 88 Stat. 1561. In 1974, Title 5, Sec. 552(b)(1) of the U.S. Code was amended to provide for the nondisclosure of matters that are "(A) specifically authorized under criteria established by an Executive order to be kept secret in the interest of national defense or foreign policy and (B) are in fact properly classified pursuant to such Executive order." In addition, the amendments added a new subsection to Sec. 552(a). Paragraph (B) of the new subsection, numbered (4), provided for judicial review *de novo* [a full and thorough consideration], specifically that a judge "may examine the contents of such agency records *in camera* [in private chambers] to determine whether such records or any part thereof shall be withheld under any of the exemptions set forth in subsection (b) of this section, and the burden is on the agency to sustain its action."

According to the Fourth Circuit, Congress intended these amendments to "overthrow" *EPA v. Mink,* 410 U.S. 73 (1972), a case which declared executive decisions about security classifications were not subject to judicial review. *Knopf,* 509 F.2d at 1367. However, the appellate court declared it preferred that plaintiffs bring questions about security classifications not to the judiciary but to the Interagency Classification Review Committee, made up of representatives from the departments of State, Defense, and Justice, the Atomic Energy Commission, the Central Intelligence Agency, and staff of the National Security Council.

Set up by section seven of Executive Order 11652, this diverse group "would not be expected to serve any parochial interest of a particular agency unless it coincided with the national interest." *Knopf, supra* at 1370. In addition, the court declared, the Review Committee had more background to deal with questions of classification than would any judge:

> If, therefore, any of the items in dispute are thought to be properly declassifiable now, there appears to be an available administrative remedy which is far more effective than any the judiciary may provide, which can function without threat to the national security and which can act within the Executive's traditional sphere of autonomy.
> *Id.*

The Court of Appeals then remanded the case to allow the parties to litigate the issue of classifiability. The plaintiffs declined to request another trial, and Marchetti and Marks published their book with 168 items appearing as blanks.

Similarly, in *Snepp v. United States,* 444 U.S. 507 (1980), a per curiam Supreme Court decision upheld the validity of CIA secrecy agreements, reversing a lower court ruling that refused to impose a "constructive trust" on a former agency employee who violated one. The CIA then recovered damages from Frank Snepp, collecting all profits from his book *Decent Interval,* which took a critical look at U.S. policy in South Vietnam.

According to the per curiam opinion:

> Snepp's contract... requires no more than a clearance procedure subject to judicial review. If Snepp, in compliance with his contract, had submitted his manuscript for review and the Agency had found it to contain sensitive material, presumably—if one accepts Snepp's present assertion of good intentions—an effort would have been made to eliminate harmful disclosures.

Absent agreement in this respect, the Agency would have borne the burden of seeking an injunction against publication.

Id. at 513.

According to the Court, it made no difference if the material in Snepp's book was not classified:

> Whether Snepp violated his trust does not depend upon whether his book actually contained classified information...The Government simply claims that, in light of the special trust reposed in him with the agreement that he signed, Snepp should have given the CIA an opportunity to determine whether the material he proposed to publish would compromise classified information or sources.
>
> *Id.* at 511.

Dissenting Justices Stevens, Brennan and Marshall believed the government was unjustly enriched by the terms of a constructive trust, saying punitive damages were a better remedy as a deterrent and punishment.

In *Haig v. Agee,* 453 U.S. 230 (1981), a former CIA employee who breached his security agreement was punished with revocation of his U.S. passport. Philip Agee published a book exposing intelligence operatives overseas while living in West Germany, where he moved to escape enforcement of his CIA prepublication review agreement. According to the opinion written by Chief Justice Burger, the Passport Act of 1926 gave the Secretary of State the authority to revoke Agee's passport in defense of national security:

> Assuming, *arguendo,* that First Amendment protections reach beyond our national boundaries, Agee's First Amendment claim has no foundation. The revocation of Agee's passport rests in part on the content of his speech: specifically, his repeated disclosures of intelligence operations and names of intelligence personnel. Long ago, however, this Court recognized that "[n]o one would question but that a government might prevent actual obstruction to its recruiting service or the publication of the sailing dates of transports or the number and location of troops..." Agee's disclosures...are clearly not protected by the Constitution. The mere fact that Agee is also engaged in criticism of the Government does not render his conduct beyond the reach of the law [citations omitted].
>
> *Id.* at 308-309.

The Classification System

In *McGehee v. Casey,* 718 F.2d 1137 (D.C. Cir. 1983), the Court of Appeals took cases involving CIA secrecy agreements one step further, considering not breaches violating the classification system but the system itself. Ralph McGehee, a former CIA agent, abided by his signed secrecy agreement. However, he sought declaratory relief against what he claimed was censorship in violation of the First Amendment, and further claimed the information in question was not properly classified anyway.

An appellate court declared the documents disputed in *McGehee* were properly classified and that the CIA could act "to protect substantial government interests by imposing reasonable restrictions on employee activities that in other contexts might be protected by the First Amendment." *Id.* at 1141. But, it conceded *Snepp* showed a balance was needed between the "interests of a government employee as a citizen to comment on matters of public concern and on employer to promote efficiency of public services." *McGehee, supra* at 1141.

The court noted, however, that "a review of relevant cases...shows that the precise standard for balancing is not that well settled." *Id.* at 1142. Therefore:

> We must accordingly establish a standard for judicial review of the CIA classification decision that affords proper respect to the individual rights at stake while recognizing the CIA's technical expertise and practical familiarity with the ramifications of sensitive information.
> *Id.*

The court hinted this balance might be struck by following procedures like those used in processing FOIA requests, where judges thoroughly examine pertinent documents in the privacy of chambers. In contrast to some FOIA actions, however, cases like *McGehee* could benefit from the adversarial process, since "both parties know the nature of the information in question. Courts should therefore strive to benefit from 'criticism and illumination by [the] party with the actual interest in forcing disclosure,' (citations omitted)." *Id.* at 1149. Judges should then:

> ...satisfy themselves from the record, *in camera* [in private chambers] or otherwise, that the CIA in fact had good reason to classify, and therefore censor, the material at issue. Accordingly, the courts should require that CIA explanations justify censorship with reasonable specificity, demonstrating a logical connection between the deleted information and the reasons for classification.
> *Id.* at 1148-1149.

Although the District of Columbia Circuit seemed to be taking a balanced approach to a thorny problem, the judges adopted somewhat divergent positions in statements following the court's opinion. Judge Patricia Wald sounded a disquieting note:

> ...neither the agency's nor our analysis takes account of any separate public right to know critical, albeit classified, facts about the activities of our intelligence agencies...It would of course be extremely difficult for judges to "balance" the public's right to know against an acknowledged security risk, and I do not believe we are currently authorized to do so. However, it seems important in view of recent revelations about past indiscretions in the name of national security, for some governmental institution, if not the classification system itself, to conduct such a balance.... Economic and criminal sanctions against agents who violate the preclearance and agency classification scheme are justifiable. But with no mechanism in the system for balancing

the public's right to know with possible risks to security, those sanctions can also result in the permanent loss of information crucial to public debate. Our decision today, reflecting current restraints on our authority, cannot and does not fill the public's need for such a balance.
Id. at 1150.

The classification system considered in *McGehee* appears in Executive Order 12,065, which outlined definitions of various classifications and items subject to their categorizations. This order was updated in 1983 and remains unchallenged in court. Both the 1979 and 1983 versions classified materials under three categories.

In the 1983 order, disclosing "confidential" material would cause "damage" to national security; disclosing "secret" material would cause "serious damage" to national security; and disclosing "top secret" material would cause "exceptionally grave" damage to national security. To be subject to classification, materials could contain information about military weapons or operations; the vulnerabilities or capabilities of systems and installations; foreign affairs or intelligence operations; scientific, technological or economic matters related to national security; nuclear materials or facilities; cryptology; confidential sources and any other information the President or those designated with classification authority determine is related to national security. Executive Order No. 12,356, sec. 1.3(a), 3 C.F.R. 166, 168-169 (1983).

In contrast to the *McGehee* ruling, a different circuit court declared four years earlier that "the fact of classification of a document or documents is enough to satisfy the classification element of the offense," citing interpretations of the U.S. Code used in *Scarbeck v. United States. United States v. Boyce,* 594 F.2d 1246, 1251 (9th Cir. 1979), *cert. denied,* 444 U.S. 855 (1979). In *Boyce,* a private employee contracted to the CIA appealed his conviction of selling top secret information, on the grounds the documents he sold were improperly classified. The Ninth Circuit upheld his conviction.

Yet, despite these seeming conflicts, the Supreme Court recognized in *New York Times v. United States* that too much secrecy goes against our interest in maintaining a free and open society. Wrote Justice Potter Stewart in his concurrence:

> ...moral, political and practical considerations would dictate that a very first principle [for classifying information] would be an insistence upon avoiding secrecy for its own sake. For when everything is classified, nothing is classified, and the system becomes one to be disregarded by the cynical or the careless, and to be manipulated by those intent on self-protection or self-promotion...The hallmark of a truly effective internal security system would be the maximum possible disclosure, recognizing that secrecy can best be preserved only when credibility is truly maintained.
> *New York Times v. United States,*
> 403 U.S. at 729.

In 1985, the press aired the problems involved in classifying defense documents after a number of highly publicized cases of alleged espionage. A government task force was appointed to consider the system of classifying and accessing materials.

The United States has witnessed a vocal, and sometimes vociferous, debate about where to divide concerns about national defense from those on freedom of expression. Yet, on a basic level, most Americans agree both must be carefully guarded to preserve for our posterity the blessings that we have enjoyed.

REPORTERS' SHIELD LAWS

A Case of Confidentiality

Cast of Characters, in order of their appearance

JUDGE CHARLES BENTON DAILY, appellate court judge
JUDGE WILLIAM FORREST, appellate court judge
JUDGE ANN WILLIAMS, appellate court judge
ANDREW GREEN, attorney for *Riverview Tribune*
MICHELLE LARSON, attorney for the plaintiff, Dr. Nathan Reede

After eight people died under unusual circumstances at Riverview Memorial Hospital, *Riverview Tribune* reporter Sally Randall began a series of investigative reports about the deaths; her reports eventually led to the indictment of Dr. Nathan Reede for murder. Dr. Reede's counsel asked the court to issue a *subpoena duces tecum,* which would compel Randall to appear with her notes for pre-trial depositions. Fearing she would be asked to reveal her confidential sources, Randall refused to cooperate, claiming reporters' notes and sources are privileged and confidential. The *Tribune* reporter was held in contempt of court, given a daily fine of $500 and sentenced to an indefinite jail term. The fine and jail sentence will be rescinded when Randall complies with the court order to disclose her sources and notes. Today, Randall appears in court to appeal the contempt citation against her.

(This mock appellate hearing will feature attorneys' arguments before a three-judge panel. The arguments will rely on fewer legal citations than is usual in such proceedings, to make them understandable to lay audiences. Those playing the role of judges should freely interrupt the attorneys to ask questions. Some questions are included in the script; others should suggest themselves during the course of the forum. Since juries are not used in appellate proceedings, the audience will hear the arguments and then act as "judges for a day." Both they and those acting as judges will deliberate on the issues presented, engaging in a socratic dialogue.)

JUDGE CHARLES BENTON DAILY: The courtroom will now come to order. Before we begin, I would like to address the large audience this hearing has attracted. I intend to keep this courtroom open to the public and the press throughout the course of this hearing; but, I must warn you that any outbursts or other disturbances which would interfere with the operation of this court will not be tolerated. If any such disruptions do occur, I will be compelled to clear the courtroom and close its doors.

Mr. Green, you have moved that the contempt citation of your client be overturned. Please proceed with your case.

ANDREW GREEN: May it please the court, my name is Andrew Green, with the law firm of Adams, Jayson, and Green. My firm represents the *Riverview Tribune* and has been retained as counsel for its reporter Sally Randall. We contend Ms. Randall has properly refused to obey an improperly issued subpoena, which requested she appear for depositions in a criminal matter involving Dr. Nathan Reede. We contend said subpoena patently ignores state law and constitutes a violation of Ms. Randall's freedom of speech and of the press, guaranteed by the First Amendment of the United States Constitution.

The subpoena in question was based on information contained in Ms. Randall's newspaper series on eight unexplained deaths at Riverview Memorial Hospital. Her investigative reporting can be credited with prompting a law enforcement investigation that culminated in Dr. Nathan Reede's criminal indictment on several counts of murder.

In June, a district court judge approved a subpoena that invited Ms. Randall to appear for depositions in Dr. Reede's murder trial. She refused to comply with the subpoena, on the advise of counsel, and was then charged with contempt of court for refusing to do so. By charging Ms. Randall with contempt, the trial judge disregarded the state shield law, which provides reporters with protection of confidential news sources and other information gleaned during the course of their work. Because the shield law was ignored in this case, I submit that the subpoena was improperly issued and that enforcing it actually impinges on important First Amendment rights.

Your Honors, the press serves an important function in our society. It acts as a constitutionally mandated check on the operation of government. The importance of the press in our constitutional system is explicitly recognized by the First Amendment. The First Amendment provides protection not only for freedom of speech, but specifically for freedom of the press as well.

The debt that society owes to a free press is enormous. Instances in which it has served the public interest are legion. If not for the press, innumerable cases of official corruption would have gone unnoticed and unpunished. The public can depend, and does depend, on the press for information on what government is doing. Only through the press have we come closer to realizing the ideal of a self-governing nation, with citizens assuming an active role as an informed electorate.

Today, in the case before the court, we have yet another example of the press performing an important public service. But, instead of receiving appreciative praise for that service, Sally Randall is rewarded with a prison sentence.

This is the sequence of events that brought us into this courtroom today: Eight deaths occurred in a relatively short time at Riverview Memorial Hospital. While deaths do occur at hospitals, most times they are due to natural causes and no unusual circumstances warrant investigation. However, something was unusual about the deaths at Riverview. Relatives of the deceased felt something was wrong, but they couldn't quite put their fingers on it. Hospital officials dismissed their concerns as the usual grief and denial brought on by unexpected and tragic death.

As a reporter, Ms. Randall had no reason to suspect anything unusual; but after repeated hints that something was amiss, she nonetheless took time to investigate. Her investigations revealed discrepancies between the hospital records and the recollections of hospital personnel, enough to indicate the deaths of those eight persons did not result naturally from their treatment. It became apparent to many connected with the case that murder was a likely explanation. Ms. Randall's reports led police to launch their own probe into the deaths, resulting in the grand jury investigation and indictment of Dr. Reede. I believe we can say law enforcement officials would not have investigated this suspicious situation if it weren't for the vigilance and persistence of the press.

As is evident from the facts, it was the police investigation that resulted directly in Dr. Reede's criminal indictment. There is no cause for the courts or defense counsel to impose a special burden on Sally Randall. The Reede case should now proceed like any other murder trial. Sally Randall acted as we would want any citizen to act: She discovered information about a possible crime and turned it over to the police. But, unlike the average citizen, Ms. Randall didn't telephone the police or go to the police station with her information — she reported it in a newspaper. Because this information appeared in a public document, Dr. Reede's defense has access to the same information as do the police, namely the newspaper reports. Just as defense attorneys cannot request depositions from people who come forward to report a possible crime or from anonymous tipsters, they should not impose a special burden on a member of the press. If someone gives information to the police that leads to a criminal investigation and indictment, we don't allow defense counsel to harass them. We know this would discourage citizens from reporting information important to the police and fulfilling their civic duties. The same reasoning applies here, as we realize the "chilling effect" this sort of subpoena has on the investigatory ardor of a free press.

The press can only fulfill its important societal function if it is unfettered by constraints like this court proceeding. The First Amendment prevents the press from being an investigatory arm of government or aides to counsel for criminal defendants. It could not do so and remain free. To force journalists to become investigators for government or defense attorneys would impose a heavy burden on their ability to be unbiased communicators. Further, this burden would discourage the press from actively reporting on matters of public importance, since at any time they could be roped into legal entanglements: either to give information to parties in a suit or to fight contempt charges and jail terms for not doing so.

Instead, the press must maintain an independent role, so it can stick its nose into places others cannot or will not go. Only then can it bring forth information from all sides of an issue, and let the public decide those issues for itself. This "watchdog" privilege is protected by the First Amendment, to insulate the press from being used by others to further their own ends.

JUDGE ANN WILLIAMS: Mr. Green, don't defendants who face possible imprisonment have a constitutional right to a fair trial? And thus, shouldn't we allow them to pursue any information that might help them mount a full defense, as guaranteed by the Sixth Amendment of the Constitution?

GREEN: While every criminal defendant has a right to a fair trial, that right cannot be considered a ticket to trample equally important press rights. The defense counsel in *State v. Reede,* in effect, wants to make Sally Randall another investigator in the defendant's employ, using the products of her diligent investigation of the Riverview Hospital deaths. It would be one thing if Ms. Randall were an eyewitness or had some independent knowledge of the events that led to these criminal charges. Our system of justice guarantees a fair trial by assuring defendants have the opportunity to face their accusers. But Sally Randall is *not* the accuser, and she is not a witness. The information she uncovered about the case could just as easily be obtained through diligent effort by the defendant and his counsel. The information that Ms. Randall wants to keep confidential will not be part of the prosecution's case, unless the prosecution manages to uncover that information on its own. In effect, both defense counsel and government prosecutors have gotten all they should out of Sally Randall—what they read in her articles in the *Riverview Tribune.*

In addition, the state shield law specifically applies to the circumstances of this case before the court. That law protects a reporter from being compelled to reveal sources. It furthers the First Amendment's goal of a free press, by assuring news sources remain confidential and information continues to flow freely. If we force reporters like Ms. Randall to turn over their notes and sources, those who have information that should be public will not use journalists as a conduit for that information. They'll be too fearful that reporters-turned-informers will expose them to recriminations and prosecutions. Depriving the press of such a shield sends a message to those who are aware of improper activity that they want to report:

It's better to go along than to rock the boat — even if you suspect the activity is criminal. Subpoenaing reporters and their notes is the quickest way to dry up sources who might want to set the system aright but want to do so anonymously. The resulting "chilling" effect on newsgathering caused by the loss of these news sources would be astounding.

The issues at stake here are by no means new or unusual. This case remakes an ancient claim for the sort of societal and judicial respect for confidential relationships that is unconditionally granted to lawyers, doctors, and clergymen. The press deserves this protection as well. Numerous cases exist where a journalist has refused to divulge sources during grand jury questioning. In a 1980 New Jersey case, the reporter's shield law was upheld when the prosecutor failed to prove that the information sought was unavailable from other sources. Courts in New York, New Jersey and Tennessee have accorded journalists absolute privileges under their shield laws, absent a conflicting constitutional right.

JUDGE WILLIAMS: I have to ask you again. Doesn't the right to a fair trial amount to a conflicting constitutional right? The Constitution protects the defendant's right to a fair trial, not the prosecutor's.

GREEN: The Constitution's fair trial guarantee doesn't conflict with Ms. Randall's First Amendment rights in this situation, because she doesn't have any direct knowledge of information in the case. Defense counsel is being lazy: They don't want to go through the effort of digging up leads and investigating them. Instead, they prefer someone else do it for them for free.

But, by compelling a reporter to do their research for them, defense attorneys are violating the state shield law and Ms. Randall's First Amendment rights. This is the core of this appeal. I submit to the court that the contempt charges lodged against Ms. Randall, her fine and jail sentence should be lifted. Although the police investigation would never have re-opened without Ms. Randall's articles, defense attorneys should not try to use those articles as a springboard for building their case. Counsel for the defendant has failed to offer any evidence — for there is none — that the information it seeks cannot be obtained in a manner less destructive to First Amendment interests. I respectfully ask this court vacate the decision of the lower court.

JUDGE DAILY: Thank you, Mr. Green. Ms. Larson, please present your argument now.

MICHELLE LARSON: Your Honors, my name is Michelle Larson from the law firm of Harding, Applebee, and Larson. I am an attorney for Dr. Nathan Reede. Normally, actions such as the one we are considering, which attempts to vacate a court order, must be filed against the state or the authority that issued the initial order. But because my client's interests in this matter are substantial, I asked the prosecutor's office for permission to defend this appeal. They agreed.

As you know, in June, Judge Arnold Williamson approved a subpoena requesting Sally Randall appear at a deposition in connection with the criminal murder trial of Dr. Reede. The judge, after carefully deliberating for a full month, decided that the notes and sources Randall collected during her investigation for the *Riverview Tribune* were relevant and important to the doctor's defense of the charges brought against him.

Randall appeared at the deposition, but she refused to disclose any information or sources and hid behind the state shield law for protection.

JUDGE WILLIAM FORREST: Isn't there validity to Randall's claim, when she says that the shield law protects reporters from being compelled to reveal confidential information or sources?

LARSON: While the shield law does provide protection to reporters generally, in this case, a countervailing right must take precedence over the security the shield affords reporters. The state constitution gives criminal defendants the right to compel testimony to assure them that all relevant information concerning their cases is before the court. In addition, the Sixth Amendment to the United States Constitution guarantees those defendants a fair trial. In the face of these important constitutional rights, the state shield law must yield.

Precedent shows that shield laws have always bowed to the more absolute laws of state and federal constitutions. There is no constitutional provision that guarantees the confidentiality of news sources. But there is a constitutional right for those accused of crimes. It would be sorely violated by affording absolute confidentiality to reporters' sources.

And, more than abstract principle is at stake in this case. If convicted, Dr. Reede stands to lose his liberty. Because of the dire nature of his possible punishment, our concern for him should be greater than what we have for a news source whose name might be revealed. In fact, common sense and common decency dictate that a defendant's right to a fair trial is the most important constitutional interest to be protected by any court. That is what is at issue here, not the unbridled freedom of the press.

No right to the confidentiality of sources is guaranteed in either the state or federal constitutions. In addition, there is no right to confidentiality that can be derived from common law. The press cannot say it is analogous to lawyers, doctors, or clergymen. Those who practice these ancient professions require several years of special schooling and training before they receive the legal protection of confidential work relations. The "press," on the other hand, is a tenuous term for a formless group. Anyone with a printing press or a copying machine can make a legitimate claim to being a member of the "press." The Supreme Court has repeatedly refused to give the press special treatment beyond that enjoyed by private citizens, and it has even rejected giving the press a qualified privilege of confidentiality.

Still, the press is hardly left unprotected. While there is no unqualified press privilege, the courts have held that the press cannot be forced into "wholesale" disclosure. A party seeking disclosure must prove that the information requested goes to the heart of its claim. In criminal cases like this one, the information must be shown to be important to the defense. Judge Williamson was satisfied the "heart of the claim" requirement was met in Dr. Reede's case.

In a 1977 case, which indicates how other courts have ruled in situations like this, John Hammerly, a reporter for the *Sacramento Union*, refused to turn over his tapes and notes to a grand jury convened in a murder investigation. A California court found Hammerly's refusal infringed upon the defendant's right to a fair trial and denied that defendant the due process of law. This sort of ruling has been the most frequent result in courts across the land.

Based on the precedents of similar cases, Randall should be required to produce her notes and reveal her sources, to the extent that they are relevant to mounting a proper defense to answer the charges brought against Dr. Reede. The decision of the court that found Randall in contempt of court should be affirmed. The privilege the press lays claim to is both unnecessary and in conflict with important constitutional rights. A press privilege exists neither in common law nor in the Constitution. The only form of protection that exists for news sources is a statutory one, and it must be put aside in this case to conform to constitutional mandates. Thank you.

JUDGE DAILY: Mr. Green, do you have anything to say in rebuttal?

GREEN: Yes, your Honor. I want to impress upon you that this court was not convened to consider a fair trial issue. No one here is trying to deny anyone a fair trial. No admissible evidence is being withheld, and Ms. Randall is not a party to any suit; she is not anyone's accuser, and she will not be a witness.

Instead, this court was convened to consider a First Amendment case. Counsel for Dr. Reede would have us sacrifice the First Amendment to go on a wild fishing expedition—on mere claims that it is *possible* additional evidence *may* be produced by rummaging through a reporter's notes and harassing her confidential sources.

If the state shield law was unclear before this case made news, its intent cannot be in doubt today. The state legislature, shortly after this case came to court, amended and clarified the shield law to protect reporters in just these circumstances. The legislature, as the debates on the floor indicate, was reacting to the lower court's contempt citation against Ms. Randall. Yes, the new law can only apply prospectively; but it would be a mockery of justice to ignore the legislature's clear statement that the shield law is necessary to give meaning to the First Amendment's press protections.

JUDGE DAILY: Are there any further points?

LARSON: Your Honors, I would like to make just one point: that the citizens of this country have been constitutionally guaranteed the right to due process of law. This guarantee provides an assurance that our system of justice will work. Giving the defendant the opportunity to question an individual who has information relevant to his defense is a matter of due process. It is essential to ensure a fair trial, as provided by the Sixth Amendment. I respectfully request that the contempt appeal by denied.

JUDGE DAILY: Thank you, counselors. *(Judge Daily speaks to the audience.)* Now, we will do something unusual for an appellate hearing. All of you in the audience today will be sworn in as judges for this case and asked to participate in the deliberations. Let's start with a question for our new judicial colleagues. Should Sally Randall be forced to make her notes and sources available to Dr. Reede's defense?

(Judge Daily calls on members of the audience to discuss the case. All three judges should participate in questioning the audience, using hypothetical situations to test the limits of those opinions as well as examples from actual judicial decisions in this area. The socratic discussion should end by polling the audience on the express issue before the court, whether or not the contempt citation should be upheld.)

Memorandum on Legal Issues

Reporters' Shield Laws

Judges often have the troublesome task of balancing freedom of the press with a defendant's right to supoena witnesses to assure a fair trial under the Sixth Amendment. Journalists argue that without a protection for confidential news contacts and information, their ability to gather news would be hampered or destroyed by the loss of sources. The press claims a right to confidentiality under the First Amendment and, in 26 states, under reporters' shield laws.

Press freedom has always occupied an important place in our constitutional pantheon. Justice Hugo Black wrote, "the only conclusion supported by history is that the unqualified prohibitions laid down by the framers were intended to give liberty of the press, as to other liberties, the broadest scope that could be countenanced in an orderly society." *Bridges v. California,* 314 U.S. 252, 264-265 (1941).

But, in *Branzburg v. Hayes,* 408 U.S. 665 (1972), the Supreme Court voted 5-4 to reject a journalist's efforts to invoke a First Amendment-based privilege against forced disclosure to a grand jury. While recognizing that newsgathering is constitutionally protected, the Court determined that "requiring newsmen to appear and testify before state or federal grand juries [does not] abridge...the freedom of speech and press guaranteed by the First Amendment. *Id.* at 667. The determination was based on the competing interests of law enforcement. The Court noted:

> Only where news sources themselves are implicated in crime or possess information relevant to the grand jury's task need they or the reporter be concerned about grand jury subpoenas. Nothing before us indicates that a large number or percentage of all confidential news sources falls into either category and would in any way be deterred by our holding that the Constitution does not, as it never has, exempt the newsman from performing the citizen's normal duty of appearing and furnishing information relevant to the grand jury's task.
> *Id.* at 691.

The Court did leave open the door to affording reporter's a limited privilege under special conditions: "Official harassment of the press undertaken not for purposes of law enforcement but to disrupt a reporter's relationship with his news sources would have no justification." *Id.* at 708.

155

In addition, Justice Lewis Powell's concurrence noted government could not use the news media as an additional investigative arm, or "a motion to quash and an appropriate protective order may be entered." *Id.* at 710.

Justice Potter Stewart, for the four dissenting justices, stressed the First Amendment interest in preserving confidentiality: "The reporter's constitutional right to a confidential relationship with his source stems from the broad societal interest in a full and free flow of information to the public." *Id.,* at 725. A right to publish implies a right to gather news, he contended, and indicated the standard that should be applied:

> The government must (1) show that there is probable cause to believe that the newsman has information that is clearly relevant to a specific probable violation of law; (2) demonstrate that the information sought cannot be obtained by alternative means less the destructive of First Amendment rights; and (3) demonstrate a compelling and overriding interest in the information.
> *Id.* at 743.

Despite his minority status, Justice Stewart's standard has greatly influenced lower courts. See, *e.g., In re Petroleum Products Antitrust Litigation,* 680 F.2d 5 (2d Cir. 1982) and *U.S. v. Hubbard,* 493 F.Supp. 202 (D.D.C. 1979).

Other courts have relied on Justice Powell's concurrence to recognize a journalistic privilege in a variety of contexts. But their decisions are divided about the extent to which a qualified First Amendment privilege should be recognized in a criminal trial. When disclosure is sought by a criminal defendant, courts tend to provide a conditional privilege. See *State of Vermont v. St. Peter,* 132 Vt. 266, 270-71, 315 A.2d 254, 255-56 (Vt. Sup. 1974) and *Brown v. Commonwealth of Virginia,* 214 Va. 755, 757, 204 S.E.2d 429, 431 (Va. Sup.), *cert. denied,* 419 U.S. 966 (1974), recognizing journalists' privilege and imposing a standard similar to that suggested by Justice Stewart's dissent.

While rejecting a constitutionally based confidentiality privilege, the *Branzburg* Court did specifically recognize that Congress and state legislatures could write a statutory privilege "as narrow or broad as deemed necessary." *Id.* at 706. Although Congress has not responded with legislation, many states have.

New York provides absolute confidentiality to reporters, with state courts ruling the shield law protects sources and notes in both civil and criminal cases, whether the communication is confidential or not. *People v. Iannaccone,* 447 N.Y.S.2d 996 (N.Y. Sup. 1982). A 1982 New Jersey case determined its shield law provides an absolute privilege against disclosing notes, memorandums, rough drafts, editorial comments, sources and other information sought by a defamation plaintiff. *Resorts International, Inc. v. NJM Association,* 89 N.J. 212, 445 A.2d 395 (N.J. Sup. 1982). See also, *Wilkins v. Kalla,* 118 Misc.2d 34, 459 N.Y.S.2d 985 (N.Y. Sup. 1983), and *Austin v. Memphis Publishing,* 655 S.W.2d 146 (Tenn. Sup. 1983).

Although it had what was considered a strong shield law, New Jersey strengthened the statute several times in response to court decisions. The first time, it was amended as a result of *In re Bridge,* 120 N.J. 460, 295 A.2d 3 (N.J. Sup. 1972), *cert. denied,* 410 U.S. 991 (1973). A separate provision was created so that reporters forced to disclose information were not required to identify their source. This new provision made the privilege for New Jersey journalists more comprehensive.

In re Farber, 78 N.J. 259, 394 A.2d 330 (N.J. Sup. 1978), *cert. denied,* 439 U.S. 997 (1978), provided another reason for New Jersey to amend its shield law. The *Farber* case involved a *New York Times* reporter who investigated 13 unexplained deaths that occurred in 1965 at Riverdell Hospital in New Jersey. In 1975, reporter Myron Farber received a note from a Riverdell public relations consultant that questioned the suspicious circumstances surrounding the deaths. Farber began investigating the seeming mystery, and soon felt he had enough information to go to press. *The New York Times* began the series in January 1976, alleging that an unnamed "Dr. X" was responsible for the unusual deaths. At the time the series began, the case had been dropped for lack of evidence. However, shortly thereafter prosecutors reopened the case file and eventually indicted Dr. Mario Jascelevitch on charges of murder.

At the request of defense counsel, a subpoena was issued asking Farber to produce his notes, including confidential sources, to be examined *in camera* [in the judge's private chambers]. Farber appeared before the grand jury but refused to disclose any information or sources, claiming a right to withhold the information under the New Jersey shield law. However, the court determined that the requested information was probably material to Jascelevitch's case and that the state shield law had to yield before the doctor's right to a fair trial. For refusing to disclose the requested information, Farber was held in contempt of court and sent to jail indefinitely. Jascelevitch was later acquitted, and Farber was released from jail with 40 days time served. Farber was eventually pardoned.

Another New Jersey case, *State v. Boirdo,* 82 N.J. 446, 414 A.2d 14, (N.J. Sup. 1980), applied the state shield law with different results. The state supreme court quashed the defense's subpoena for a letter the prosecution's key witness wrote to a reporter. The letter allegedly revealed a contradiction and bias in the witness's testimony. The court agreed that the letter was relevant to the defense's case and that disclosing it would result in only a minimal "chilling" effect on the press. Yet, it quashed the subpoena, because the defense counsel failed to prove that alternative sources for the information were unavailable, as required by the shield law.

The current New Jersey shield law was amended in February 1980, to allow reporters to refuse to disclose information obtained during newsgathering in any judicial, legislative, or administrative proceeding, even when subpoenaed by a defendant in a criminal trial. The legislative body reasoned that "forced disclosure" would ultimately hurt society. Citizens would lose the ability to remain well-informed, which allows them to take an active part in government. The New Jersey legislature concluded that "any inhibition of flow of information by forced disclosure of confidential sources and information may be said to contravene the spirit and letter of the First Amendment guarantee of freedom of the press." D. Cohen, "Sixth Amendment Limitations on the Newsperson's Privilege: A Breach in the Shield," 13 Rutgers L.J., 364.

Some case law shows that shield laws do not always prevail. *Farr v. Superior Court,* 22 Cal. App. 3d 60, 99 Cal. Rptr. 342 (Ct. App. 1971), *cert. denied,* 409 U.S. 1011 (1972) and *Ammerman v. Hubbard Broadcasting, Inc.,* 89 N.M. 307, 551 P.2d 1354 (N.M. Sup. 1976), *cert. denied,* 436 U.S. 906 (1978), held that shield laws must yield to defendants' Sixth Amendment rights to a fair trial. In *Ammerman,* the court also ruled that the shield law violated the separation of powers clause of the state constitution, because it conflicted with the court's established rules of evidence.

The press's vulnerability in the face of forced disclosures was demonstrated in *Zurcher v. Stanford Daily,* 436 U.S. 547 (1978). Police, armed with a warrant, searched a university newspaper office for negatives, photographs and films to be used as evidence in a case arising from a student riot. The Court found the search constitutional, rejecting a Fourth Amendment argument and the student journalists' assertion that news sources would be indiscriminately revealed. The Court's sentiments were summarized by Justice Powell in his concurring opinion:

> If the framers had believed that the press was entitled to a special procedure, not available to others, when government authorities required evidence in its possession, one would have expected the terms of the Fourth Amendment to reflect that belief.
>
> *Id.,* at 569.

Congress responded to the *Zurcher* decision with the Privacy Protection Act of 1980, 42 U.S.C. Sec. 2000aa (Supp. 1980), restricting governmental search and seizure of "any work product materials possessed by a person reasonably believed to have a purpose to disseminate to the public a newspaper, book, broadcast, or other similar form of public communication...in connection with the investigation or prosecution of a criminal offense" except when the newsperson was involved in the criminal offense, when someone was threatened with death or serious injury, or when national security was at stake. The Act was engineered to require law enforcement authorities to obtain a subpoena for information they want, instead of using search warrants to enter newsrooms.

Although it protects reporters to some extent, the Privacy Protection Act avoided giving the press blanket protection: if authorities suspect that a subpoena could lead to the destruction of evidence, they may proceed without waiting for a warrant. An officer's "good faith" is also a complete defense for a civil action brought by complaining journalists in such a case.

The controversy over providing confidentiality to reporters' sources and the effect such a privilege would have on the criminal justice system remains a difficult issue for the courts. Legislatures have also wrestled with the problem. However, the National Conference of Commissioners on Uniform State Laws ended work on a proposed Uniform Shield Law, because "members could not agree on details or that a need existed." *Editor & Publisher,* Aug. 30, 1975, p. 18.

THE ZENGER TRIAL:
ITS BEGINNINGS AND LEGACY

Speaking and Writing Truth
by Robert S. Peck

The invention of the printing press carried revolutionary implications. Suddenly, speech could be mass produced and preserved over time. Ideas could be communicated to large numbers of people and not lose their power in the retelling. Books, broadsides and newspapers became popular forms of expression. To the English Crown, this was dangerous. Independently published tracts undermined royal authority by eliminating governmental control over the flow of information. Because printed materials gave them access to the minds of the realm's subjects, publishers became invested with a special authority that the Crown wanted to retain only for itself.

To combat this trend, royal authority over the press was asserted through a succession of regulatory systems, often draconian in nature. Even before the printing press, King Alfred of Wessex in the ninth century demanded that anyone found responsible for libelous statements receive "no lighter penalty than the cutting off of his tongue."

The suppression of speech, particularly printed speech, was aimed at ending criticism of the government. Critiques that were merely oral were comparatively harmless, because of their limited reach. Besides, it was virtually impossible to regulate casually spoken criticisms without secret police, or at least a society of informers. Instead, publications became the target of censorship.

In 1275, the English Parliament banned "any slanderous News...or false News or Tales where by discord or occasion of discord or slander may grow between the King and his people or the great men of the Realm...." This law effectively banished news of bad policies, corruption, governmental failures and injustice. In addition, because church and state were one, governmental criticism was also regarded as heresy or blasphemy, slighting the church as well. Criminal charges could be preferred for libel or heresy, and often both.

Because, to an Englishman, there is nothing like a good argument, strong support developed for the concept of free speech. It was, however, still limited to "safe" speech. By 1620, King James I professed his support for freedom of speech, but cautioned that state affairs "are no Theames, or subjects fit for vulgar persons, or common meetings." It was unthinkable, the king was saying, to allow commoners to speak ill of their lords.

Printing became a state matter, subject to royal fiat. The king, and later the Court of the Star Chamber in 1637, limited the number of printers and presses by subjecting all new publications to an approval process. Royal censors excised objectionable passages and arbitrarily made decisions on whether to license publications. Unlicensed publications were seized as contraband. This book-licensing authority was transferred from the Star Chamber to Parliament in 1641, until it expired in 1694.

England's "Glorious Revolution" forced King James II to abdicate in favor of William of Orange, but only under a strict set of conditions, known as the Bill of Rights of 1689. The Bill's provisions trimmed royal authority and established parliamentary sovereignty. More importantly, they led to the steady expansion of civil liberties, including freedom from arbitrary arrest and the end of press censorship. The Bill of Rights specifically protected the free speech rights of Parliament's members, retaining the royal distinction between the governors and the governed. Moreover, in a separate act, Parliament prohibited the unauthorized reporting of its proceedings, as well as criticism of anything related to government.

As censorship fell into disrepute, prosecutions for seditious libel became the favored means of controlling the press. Seditious libel was defined as "the intentional publication, without lawful excuse or justification, of written blame of any public man, or of the law, or any institution established b w." Like the rationale for censorship, the reasoning behind this prohibition against criticism of officialdom was that it would ridicule government or the governors, thereby diminishing their claims to authority. It mattered little if the published critique was true. "The greater the truth the greater the libel" was the rule of law followed, because a truthful publication was more prone to be believed and thus carry with it greater disdain for government.

English prosecutions for seditious libel were common. In 1702, for example, journalist Daniel Defoe, better know for his novels *Robinson Crusoe* and *Moll Flanders,* was imprisoned and pilloried for his satiric attack on the Church of England for its oppression of nonconforming clergy.

First Printing Press Arrives in America

Locksmith Stephen Day became the first printer in America in 1639 when he purchased a press that survived the trans-Atlantic voyage from England but whose owner did not. Thirty years after the arrival of Day's purchase, there were still no printing presses in the Carolinas, Maryland, New Jersey, New York or Virginia. The absence of presses was not mourned by colonial officials. Virginia's governor, Sir William Berkeley, wrote in 1671:

...I thank God, there are no free schools nor *printing* [in Virginia], and I hope we shall not have these [for a] hundred years; for *learning* has brought disobedience, and heresy, and sects into the world, and *printing* has divulged them, and libels against the best government. God keep us from both.

Virginia was later to boast some of America's greatest defenders of both education and a free press. James Madison, father of the First Amendment, took a position opposite to the antediluvian view of Berkeley. "Learned institutions," Madison said, "ought to be favorite objects with every free people. They throw that light over the public mind which is the best security against crafty and dangerous encroachments on the public liberty." He added, "What spectacle can be more seasonable, than that of liberty and learning, each leaning on the other for their mutual and surest support?"

However, despite its later well-known champions of liberty, seventeenth-century Virginia was unrelentingly hostile to free speech and a free press. The House of Burgesses punished libels directly, rather than relying on the courts. In 1660, a man who complained about taxes was jailed for "scandalous, mutinous, and seditious" language. A man who in 1682 published the colonial laws without a license was forced to post a bond of 100 pounds, forfeitable if he ever printed anything again. Regularly, individuals who printed objectionable materials were called to the House to kneel and beg forgiveness, then be imprisoned.

Press Freedom Challenged in Criminal Trial

Parliamentary "justice" was not restricted to Virginia, but common throughout the colonies. The courts were well-used too. John Peter Zenger's mentor, William Bradford, was the defendant in one of the earliest American criminal trials to challenge press freedom. Bradford was Pennsylvania's first printer. His first publication, an almanac, was censored by officials while still a manuscript. He ran afoul of the governor and Council again when he printed a copy in 1689 of the "Frame of Government" at the request of a councillor but in violation of a six-year old act prohibiting the publication of colonial laws.

Bradford was fined 500 pounds and admonished against publishing again without official permission. He went to England to escape Pennsylvania's censorship, but returned only to run into trouble with the law again—this time for publishing the political pamphlets of a separatist Quaker faction. Bradford's press was seized, and he and his Quaker employers were charged with seditious libel. They were convicted without an opportunity to defend themselves by a court of eight magistrates, six of whom had been criticized in the published tracts.

While the others were fined five pounds apiece, Bradford and one other demanded a jury trial as guaranteed by the Magna Carta. Bradford's case presaged many of the arguments made at the Zenger trial years later. After spending four months in jail, Bradford represented himself at his trial and unsuccessfully challenged two jurors for failing to be impartial. He also argued that the jurors should judge not just the fact of publication, but also whether the tract was indeed seditious and, even so, whether it weakened the hands of the authorities. His argument failed, and the prosecution concentrated on proving Bradford printed the offending pamphlet.

Inexplicably, the judge, who rejected the argument that the jury could judge both fact *and* law, instructed the jury to decide whether Bradford was the printer *and* whether the tract was seditious. A deadlocked jury sent Bradford back to jail for nearly a year to await a second trial.

Instead of returning to court, Bradford won his release when William Penn's charter was suspended and New York Governor Benjamin Fletcher took control of Pennsylvania. Fletcher had Bradford's printing press released as well, because he believed New York needed an official printer. Bradford's imprisonment transformed him into a royal loyalist and his *New-York Gazette* became the governor's official newspaper. Others who survived similar trials in early America followed similar patterns.

First American Newspaper Published

The first true American newspaper was published in 1690 by Benjamin Harris, an exiled London printer with a reputation as a subversive. The newspaper, *Publick Occurrences, Both Foreign and Domestick,* was banned after its first issue for violating licensing restrictions and for promoting scandal. Harris' offenses were reporting truthfully about an aborted English attack on the French and the savagery of Britain's Indian allies and revealing that the French king had taken liberties with the prince's wife. The newspaper's banishment discouraged others from printing reports with a potential to offend. The next American newspaper, the *Boston News-Letter,* didn't appear until 1704, but enjoyed a 15-year monopoly by clearing all copy in advance with the governor. As a result, it was very dull.

The next newspaper rebel in the colonies was James Franklin, who started his *New England Courant* in 1721 as a lively, readable and unlicensed publication. His stinging accusation of governmental ineffectiveness against pirates resulted in a contempt charge and a jail sentence of one month. Unchastened, the newly freed Franklin attacked the legislature for jailing him, only to be ordered never to publish again without license. Franklin circumvented the order by promoting his apprentice-brother to the position of publisher. The new publisher, Benjamin Franklin, left the *Courant* after a year for Philadelphia, where he began an illustrious career as an American statesman by starting as the journalist-publisher of the *Pennsylvania Gazette.* Without Benjamin, James Franklin became less rebellious and took a job as a government printer in Rhode Island, where he founded the colony's first newspaper.

Zenger Becomes Object of Celebrated Trial

Of all the cases in colonial America to test the concept of a free press, the most celebrated was that of John Peter Zenger. The case had no continuing legal significance, but provided an inspirational legacy that continues today. Zenger was a German who immigrated to colonial New York when he was 13. He became William Bradford's apprentice shortly after his arrival in the New World. He became a master printer whose graphic skills exceeded that of his mentor. He left Bradford's shop at the age of 21, only to return a partner after a stint as Maryland's official printer. Zenger never had any formal schooling and made no pretense of being a writer, only a printer.

When he was thirty, Zenger struck out on his own. His shop was patronized by a small group of New Yorkers who were leading members of the bar: Chief Justice Lewis Morris, Lewis Morris, Jr., James Alexander and William Smith. He published their political broadsides and pamphlets. When the colonial governor, William Cosby, removed Chief Justice Morris from office after the supreme court ruled against the government in a matter, Morris engaged Zenger to publish a pamphlet with his side of the controversy.

Flushed with the success of that pamphlet, Zenger's distinguished patrons returned to his shop to persuade him to publish an opposition newspaper for which they would anonymously write articles. Zenger was only too happy to oblige. A newspaper represented a steady demand for the skills of a printer and could bring the shop a profit.

On November 5, 1733, the first issue of Zenger's *New-York Weekly Journal* appeared. The newspaper was filled with essays on liberty and attacks detailing the corruption and incompetence of Governor Cosby. The *Journal* was almost immediately popular, since Cosby was not, and the articles were written with wit and style.

The attacks did not sit well with the governor, who ordered the new chief justice, James DeLancey, to convene a grand jury to bring Zenger to trial for libel. When this effort in January 1734 failed, DeLancey tried again in October with the same results. In addressing the grand jury, DeLancey declared, "...it is high Time to put a Stop to them [the libels];...must not these Things end in Sedition, if not timely prevented?"

On October 17, 1734, the General Assembly entered the controversy. Assemblyman Philip Cortlandt, a Cosby loyalist, enumerated charges against the *Journal*, calling it "scurrilous" and "tending to alienate the Affections of the People of this Province from His Majesty's Government, to raise Seditions and Tumults among the People of the Province, and to fill their Minds with a Contempt of His Majesty's Government...."

Zenger's Newspaper Burned

A resolution, subsequently tabled, was introduced to have copies of Zenger's newspaper brought into the Council as evidence and "burnt by the Hands of the common Hangman," to authorize a gubernatorial proclamation that carried with it "a Promise of Reward for the Discovery of the Authors or Writers of these Seditious Libels," and to demand that the printer be prosecuted. Later, the resolution was passed in amended form to authorize the burning of the *Journal*. The newspaper was burned in a public square by the sheriff's "own Negroe." In addition, Cosby offered a 50-pound reward for the identification of the authors of the *Journal* articles.

Zenger was then jailed on a warrant signed by the clerk of the Governor's Council while another grand jury met and refused to indict him. The last issue of the *Journal* before Zenger's arrest addressed the freedom of expression that was at issue. It said:

> Without freedom of thought there can be no such thing as wisdom, and no such thing as public liberty; without freedom of speech, which is the right of every man, as far as by it he does not hurt or control the right of another; and this is the only check it ought to suffer, and the only bounds it ought to know... [there is no such thing as freedom]

While Zenger was in prison, his wife Anna took over the responsibilities of publisher and kept the newspaper going.

On November 17, 1734, Attorney General Richard Bradley issued an "information," a form of indictment that doesn't require grand jury action, charging Zenger "for printing and publishing several Seditious Libels."

Zenger was not permitted visitors during the early part of his confinement. He steadfastly refused to reveal the authors of the articles in his newspaper. James Alexander, a former attorney general and principal author of the offending articles in the *Journal,* and William Smith, a future attorney general and New York supreme court justice, took on Zenger's defense. They argued vigorously for a reasonable bail, but failed to reduce the 400-pound figure that was set. Zenger's net worth was only 40 pounds, making it impossible for him to make bail. He was to remain in jail nine months awaiting trial.

Zenger's lawyers then sought to remove Chief Justice DeLancey and Justice Frederick Philipse from the case by arguing that their commissions were defective and that they thus held office illegally. For the affrontery of challenging the court, Alexander and Smith were disbarred. The removal of the two lawyers from the rolls of the bar sent a signal to other advocates that a zealous defense of Zenger would not be tolerated. The court then appointed John Chambers, an inexperienced lawyer known as a Cosby partisan, to represent Zenger at a trial set for August 4.

Normally, jurors in colonial New York were chosen from a randomly selected group of 48 from the Freeholders Book. However, the court clerk tried to rig the jury in Zenger's case with a pre-selected list of 48 of the governor's friends and allies. After Zenger's supporters objected, the court permitted the usual practice to prevail, probably assuming that even an impartial jury could not find for Zenger.

Trial Attracts Large Crowd

For Zenger's trial, an overflow crowd filled the courtroom at the corner of New York's Broad and Wall Streets where Federal Hall, later to be George Washington's inauguration site, now stands. DeLancey and Philipse, in flowing white wigs and red robes, arrived to preside at the trial. Attorney General Bradley charged Zenger with:

> printing and publishing a false, scandalous, and seditious Libel, in which his Excellancy the Governor of this Province, who is the King's immediate Representative here, is greatly and unjustly scandalized, as a Person that has no Regard to Law nor Justice; [and] with much more, as will appear upon reading the Information.

Chambers made a standard reply in Zenger's behalf, essentially reminding the jury that the attorney general had the burden to prove that Zenger was responsible for the publication.

Suddenly, there was great commotion among the spectators as a man dramatically stood up and tossed off his coat. Andrew Hamilton, the most celebrated lawyer in the colonies, surprised all but a few of Zenger's supporters by rising to appear in the printer's defense. Zenger's former lawyers had secretly arranged for Hamilton to come to New York from his home in Philadelphia, just in time for the trial. Hamilton, nearly 80 years old, had served with distinction as attorney general of Pennsylvania and speaker of its assembly.

Though Hamilton came to New York as an advocate of the free press and is best remembered for that role, he once was on the other side of the issue. While in the Pennsylvania Assembly, he called Andrew Bradford, the son of Zenger's mentor, to the bar of the legislature for publishing official records without prior permission.

The surprise of Hamilton's appearance was soon eclipsed by the surprise of his tactics. He immediately admitted the fact of publication but added that it was "supported with Truth." His strategy had been devised by Alexander, Zenger's original attorney.

Bradley jumped on the admission. He said, "...as Mr. Hamilton has confessed the Printing and Publishing these Libels, I think the Jury must find a Verdict for the King; for supposing them true, the Law says that they are not less libellous for that; nay indeed the Law says, their being true is an Aggravation of the Crime."

To ignore the truth in matters of libel, Hamilton replied, was to return to the "wickedness" of the Star Chamber. It is "the falsehood [that] makes the Scandal, and both make the Libel.... Mr. Attorney [General] has now only to prove the Words false, in order to make us Guilty."

When Bradley objected to shifting the burden of proof, Hamilton offered instead to prove the truth of the publication. DeLancey interrupted, "The Law is clear, That you cannot justify a Libel."

Hamilton replied with what may have been his best debating point, even if it failed as an argument. "I know it is said," he answered, *"That Truth makes a Libel the more provoking, and therefore the Offence is the greater, and consequently the Judgment should be the heavier."* But, he argued, without proof of the truth of the publications, the judges would not know how severe a punishment to mete out. "For, would it not be a sad Case, if the Judges, for want of a due Information, should chance to give as secure a Judgment against a Man for writing or publishing a Lie, as for writing or publishing a Truth?" he said with a tinge of irony.

Though evidence of truth and further argument on the point was not permitted by the judges, Hamilton had made his point to the jury that he stood ready and able to prove the truth of what had been printed. He bolstered the point by addressing the jury for the first time. "Then Gentlemen of the Jury," he said, "it is to you we must now appeal.... The [Law] supposes you to be summoned, *out of the Neighbourhood where the Fact is alledged to be committed*; and the Reason of your being taken out of the Neighbourhood is, *because you are supposed to have the best Knowledge of the Fact that is to be tried."*

Originally, the function of the jury was closer to that of witnesses. When an individual was accused of a crime, his neighbors were gathered to judge him since they were the most likely to have independent knowledge of the events leading to the accusation. Hamilton was referring to this established tradition when he asked the jury to reach a conclusion based on facts not in evidence. He reminded the jury that he had been prepared, though denied the opportunity, to prove the truth of what had been written. He said, *"That the suppressing of Evidence ought always to be taken for the strongest Evidence."*

The facts, Hamilton told the jury, "are notoriously known to be true; and therefore in your Justice lies our Safety." In his summation to the jury, Hamilton added:

> Men who injure and oppress the People under their Administration provoke them to cry out and complain; and then make that very Complaint the Foundation for new Oppressions and Prosecutions. I wish I could say there were no Instances of this Kind. But to conclude; the Question before the Court and you, Gentlemen of the Jury, is not of small nor private Concern, it is not the Cause of a poor Printer, nor of *New-York* alone, which you are now trying: No! It may in its Consequence, affect every Freeman that lives under a British Government on the main of *America*. It is the best Cause. It is the

Cause of Liberty; and I make no Doubt but your upright Conduct, this Day, will not only entitle you to the Love and Esteem of your Fellow-Citizens; but every Man who prefers Freedom to a Life of Slavery will bless and honour You, as Men who have baffled the Attempt of Tyranny; and by an impartial and uncorrupt Verdict, have laid a noble Foundation for securing to ourselves, our Posterity, and our Neighbours, That, to which Nature and the Laws of our Country have given us a Right, — The Liberty — both of exposing and opposing arbitrary Power (in these Parts of the World, at least) by speaking and writing Truth.

Jury Acquits Zenger

The jury left for only a short time, returning a verdict of not guilty. The victory was celebrated with cheers, the firing of shipboard guns in salute and a dinner in Hamilton's honor. The Zenger story was preserved by the publication in 1736 of *A Brief Narrative of the Case & Tryal of John Peter Zenger*. It purported to be a transcript of the case written by Zenger himself, though it was probably ghost-written by James Alexander. In addition, the Morris family passed the tale of Zenger down through the generations. Gouverneur Morris, grandson of Lewis Morris and the individual responsible for the final arrangement and wording of the U.S. Constitution, said at the time of the American Revolution, "The trial of Zenger in 1735 was the morningstar of that liberty which subsequently revolutionized America."

The trial's significance lay in the fact that it coincided with and enhanced a growing public appetite for liberty. Zenger's acquittal proved that one could speak his mind, take on the authorities and succeed. The trial was an undeniable symbol that freedom to criticize government was a fundamental element of liberty and the right to publish the criticisms was necessary to make that freedom meaningful. Of the trial's result, the *Philadelphia Gazette* said, "if it is not law, it is better than law, it ought to be law, and will always be law wherever justice prevails."

Though truth occasioned Zenger's acquittal and is now accepted as an absolute defense to libel charges, the trial did not have precedential value. While acting as a psychological barrier to authorities from bringing further prosecutions for seditious libel, the Zenger trial was not followed closely by a period of legal reform. It wasn't until the state constitution of 1790 that Pennsylvania provided for truth as a defense to libel and the right of the jury to decide the defamatory nature of the words at issue. New York didn't follow suit until 1805. England was even slower in changing. Fox's Libel Act of 1782 gave juries the right to decide the harmfulness of the defendant's words, but it wasn't until Lord Campbell's Act in 1843 that truth became a defense in cases of *criminal* libel.

Zenger's victory also emboldened the press, enabling them to play an important role in preparing the public for the American Revolution and maintaining their morale through that ordeal. When Thomas Paine's *Common Sense* appeared in January 1776, it enjoyed instant popularity, selling over 120,000 copies in its first three months. Other Paine writings proved even more popular, appearing in pamphlet form and reprinted in dozens of newspapers. Newspapers were the popular medium for learning about the colonial revolt. Many Americans read the Declaration of Independence for the first time when it was published in newspapers.

The First Amendment and Beyond

The Revolutionary War was considered a victory for freedom, a component of which included a free press. When the delegates to the Constitutional Convention gathered in Philadelphia in 1787, they were mindful of the importance of a free press, despite the closed doors behind which they drafted the new Constitution. At the Convention, Roger Sherman of Connecticut helped defeat a motion to include language that "the liberty of the press should be involuably observed" by declaring it "unnecessary — [t]he power of Congress does not extend to the Press."

The antifederalists opposed the ratification of the Constitution, in part, because it contained no bill of rights. Defenders of the Constitution, though they were later to concede the point, felt a bill of rights unnecessary. Already a signer of the Declaration of Independence and Constitution and soon to be a Supreme Court justice, James Wilson of Pennsylvania appealed for ratification against those who complained about the absence of a free press clause by saying, "it will be found that there is given to the general government no power whatsoever concerning [the press]; and no law, in pursuance of the Constitution, can possibly be enacted to destroy that liberty."

The argument in favor of the Constitution was also made through the news media of the day. The Federalist Papers, written by Alexander Hamilton, James Madison and John Jay under the shared pseudonym of "Publius," were a series of 85 essays in support of the Constitution's ratification published first in the *New York Independent Journal.* Starting in October 1787, they appeared four times a week. They were soon reprinted in newspapers throughout the country and then in pamphlet and book form. The essays provided a clear rationale and political theory for the operation of the Constitution that is still used as a guide today.

First Amendment Added to Constitution

The Constitution was ratified once the states were satisfied that a bill of rights be added. In order to avoid a second constitutional convention that might undo the work of the first, Madison introduced 15 amendments in the first Congress to serve as that bill of rights. Twelve of the amendments won congressional approval, and ten were eventually ratified by the states. Madison's fourth proposal, which eventually became the First Amendment, read in part:

> That in art. 1st, sec. 9, between cls. 3 and 4, be inserted these clauses, to wit:...
> The people shall not be deprived or abridged of their right to speak, to write, or to publish their sentiments; and *the freedom of the press, as one of the great bulwarks of liberty, shall be inviolable.*
> The people shall not be restrained from peaceably assembling and consulting for their common good; nor from applying to the Legislature by petitions, or remonstrances, for redress of their grievances...

In 1791, the Bill of Rights was ratified with the First Amendment's ringing declaration that "Congress shall make no law...abridging the freedom of speech, or of the press; or the right of the people peaceably to assemble, and to petition the Government for a redress of grievances."

Despite the battles that the founding generation fought for a brand of liberty that included a free press, political considerations were permitted to overwhelm principle from time to time. The press almost immediately became a major component of the American political system, providing the people with the information they needed to discharge their responsibilities as citizens. Newspapers began to evaluate political candidates, expose official corruption and editorialize about the policies adopted by the new government. Politicians became adept at using the news media to make their cases to the voters.

The power of the press awakened the same fear in Federalist officials that was the scourge of colonial governors—that the press, by exposing their failures, would end their hold on governmental power. The Alien and Sedition Acts of 1798 reinstated the law of seditious libel that had largely become dormant since Zenger's trial. The Sedition Act made it a crime to:

> write, print, utter or publish, or...knowingly and willingly assist or aid in writing, printing, uttering or publishing any false, scandalous and malicious writing or writings against the government of the United States, or either house of the Congress of the United States, or the President of the United States, with intent to defame the said government,...or to bring them...into contempt or disrepute; or to excite against them...the hatred of the good people of the United States, or to stir up sedition within the United States.

The Act was used by the Federalists to harrass the opposition Republicans. It was an extremely unpopular law. Twenty-five arrests and 15 indictments were made under the Act's authority. None of the cases reached the Supreme Court, though lower courts—with Federalist Supreme Court justices sitting on those courts—sustained the Act against constitutional challenge. It was not until the landmark decision in *New York Times v. Sullivan,* 376 U.S. 254 (1964), 166 years later, that the Supreme Court noted: "the great controversy over the Sedition Act of 1798...first crystallized a national awareness of the central meaning of the First Amendment.... Although the Sedition Act was never tested in this Court, the attack upon its validity has carried the day in the court of history."

The Act expired the day before Thomas Jefferson was inaugurated President in 1801 and was never renewed. Jefferson pardoned those convicted under the Act and remitted their fines.

The challenges to our First Amendment freedoms are continuous, variations on themes that have come before. The Zenger legacy shows it is ultimately up to the people to take a stand for their own liberty. Despite the First Amendment flag raised over our ship of state, our precious freedoms remain only when the people are knowledgeable about the challenges to our free expression rights and participate in resolving the issues. In *Federalist No. 84,* Alexander Hamilton recognized the crucial role of the people in maintaining a free press:

> What signifies a declaration that "the liberty of the press shall be inviolably preserved?" What is the liberty of the press? Who can give it any definition which would not leave the utmost latitude for evasion? I hold it to be impracticable; and from this, I infer, that its security, whatever fine declarations may be inserted in any constitution respecting it, must altogether depend on public opinion, and on the general spirit of the people and of the government. And here, after all, as intimated upon another occasion, must we seek for the only solid basis of all our rights.

As another Hamilton, Andrew, said at Zenger's trial:

> It is the best Cause. It is the Cause of Liberty;...and by an impartial and uncorrupt Verdict, [you will] have laid a noble Foundation for securing to ourselves, our Posterity, and our Neighbours, That, to which Nature and the Laws of our Country have given us a Right, — The Liberty — both of exposing and opposing arbitrary Power (in these Parts of the World, at least) by speaking and writing Truth.